Plus Up Phonics

Author **Joy Park**
Supervisor **LittleLambSchool**
English Research Institute

2

Author : Joy Park

Welcome to the "Plus Up Phonics Series!
Studying English phonics is necessary for learning English. But we usually think that it is not that easy to learn and even sometimes boring. Yes, right. In terms of this view, I tried to focus on stimulating English learners not to run away from learning English phonics.
Plus Up Phonics contains all of the basic and essential parts for learning English phonics and of course, it consists of many exciting and practical activities for learners.
I hope Plus Up Phonics will help your students have great confidence in English Phonics.

Supervisor : LittleLambSchool English Research Institute

"Plus Up Phonics" has everything your English learners need to begin their first step in English phonics. Because Plus Up Phonics is made of interesting word games and various phonics questions, students cannot lose their concentration on learning English phonics and also it will give a balanced knowledge of essential parts of English phonics.
We hope your students could get off on the right foot in English with the Plus Up Phonics!

About the Book

How to use Plus Up Phonics

Plus Up Phonics will allow your students to take their first right step in English.
Here are some suggestions to get the most out of this book.
Each lesson provides time allotment and homework check box for the effective and practical teaching.

Consists of Each Unit

❶ Listen and Repeat: My Dictionary
   Students listen to and reproduce the sounds they hear in words.
   Also while they find words they hear in the book, they can maintain their interests in phonics.

❷ Presentation: Short-Story, Chant, Odd Poem, and Song
   Students can look around words based on English phonics learned through four various kinds of writings: story, chant, poem and song.

❸ Let's Practice Phonics: Phonics Listening
   Students can check their understandings based on English phonics learned carefully by solving the listening questions.

❹ Pop Quiz & Mini Test
   Check the weak points and review each unit briefly.

❺ Let's Play: Phonics Activity
   Through the interesting English phonics word games, students can practice in a natural way.

❻ Homework Spot
   Homework Spot contains three kinds of phonics questions: listening, reading and writing questions. These will help your students wrap up each unit in detail.

CONTENTS

Long a, e, i sound with magic e : a-e, e-e, i-e

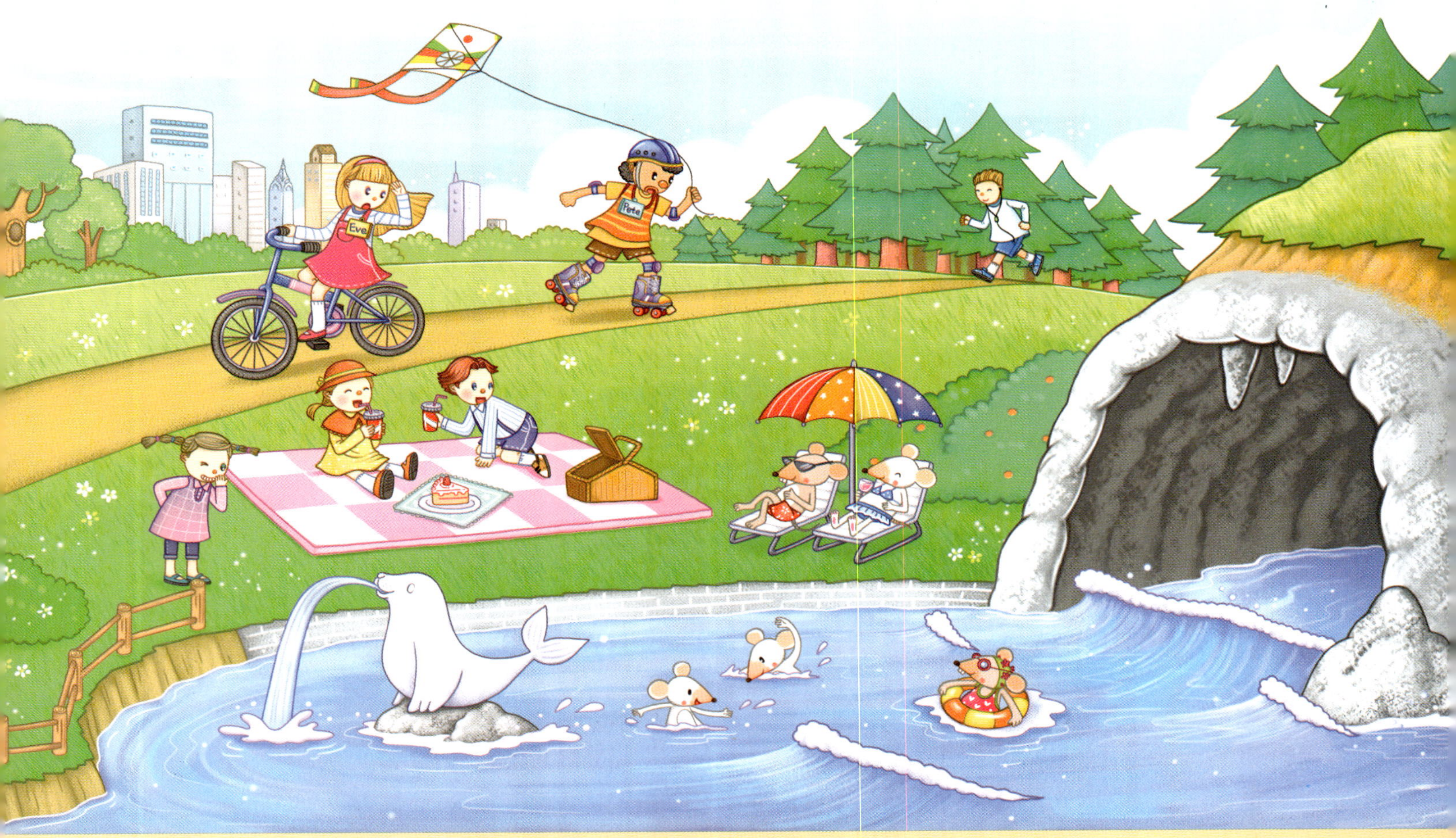

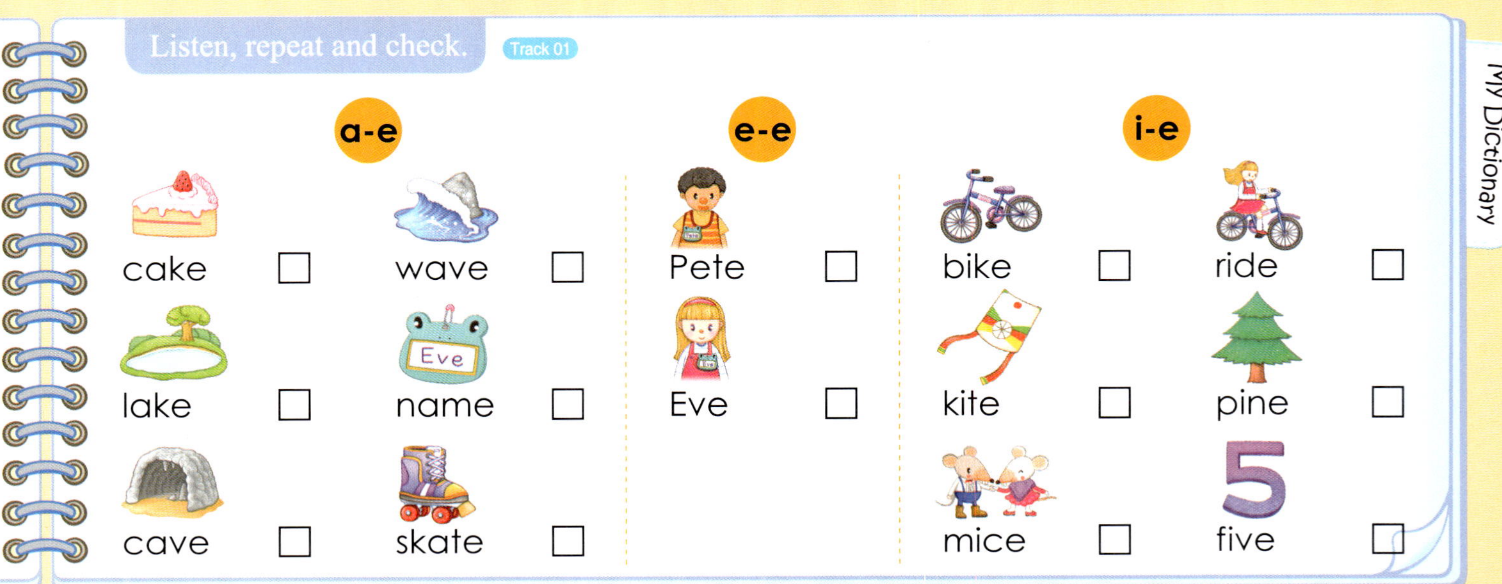

Look and find the new word, then circle.

Listen, repeat and check.   Track 01

a-e **e-e** **i-e**

cake ☐   wave ☐   Pete ☐   bike ☐   ride ☐

lake ☐   name ☐   Eve ☐   kite ☐   pine ☐

cave ☐   skate ☐   mice ☐   five ☐

Look! Ten Eyes!

 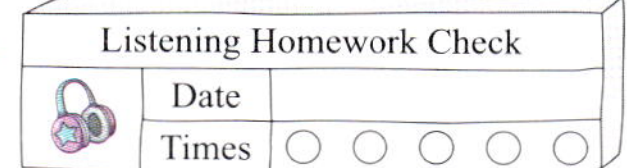

Unit 01

We go to the lake  .

Eve  has a kite  on the bike .

Pete  is on the wave  .

We go into the cave .

Look!

Ten eyes!

Five 5 mice  are on the cake  .

POP QUIZ Listen, and write the missing letters.

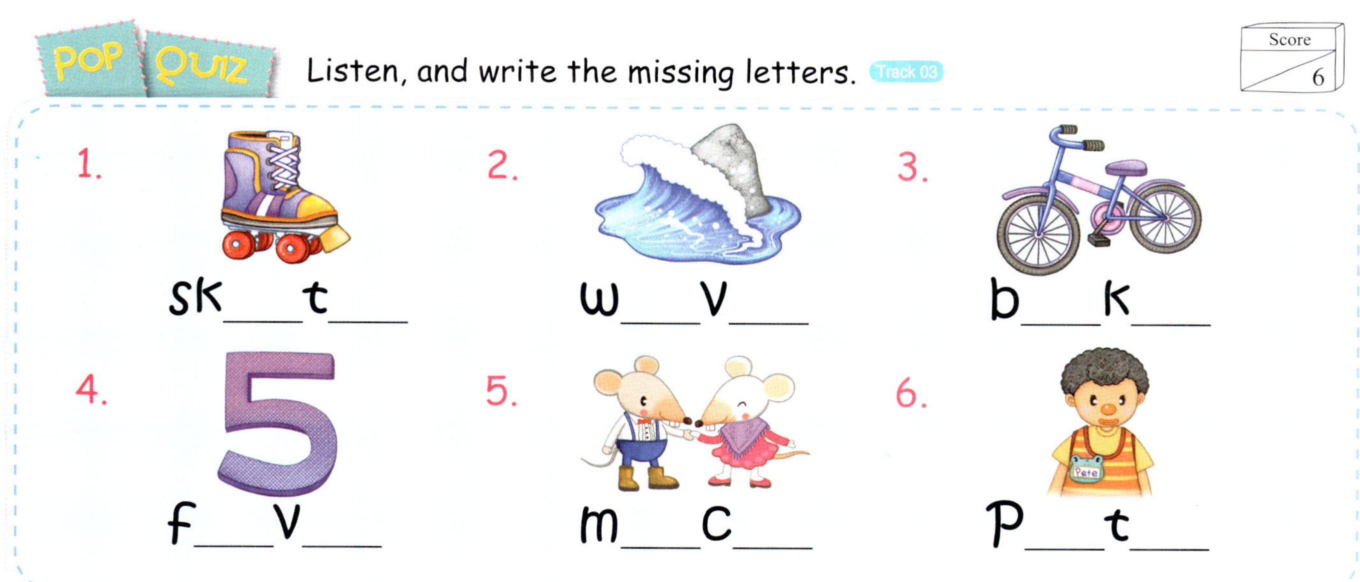

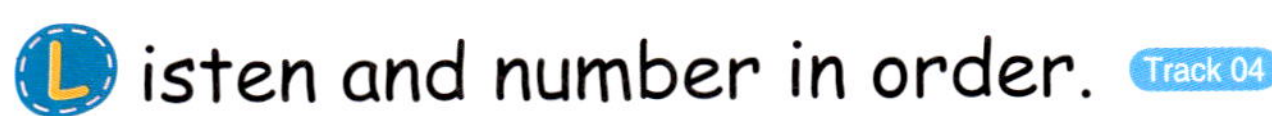 isten and number in order. Track 04

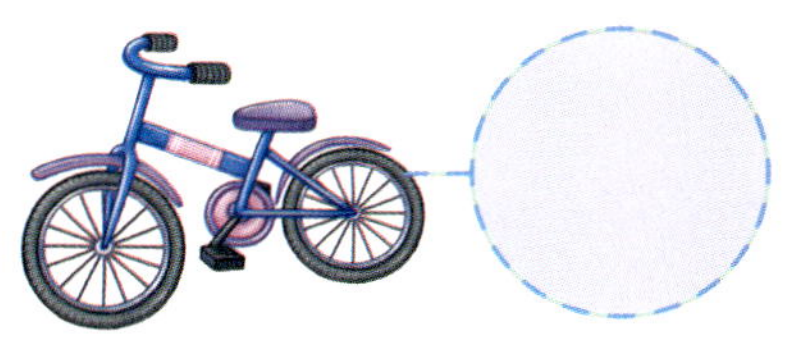 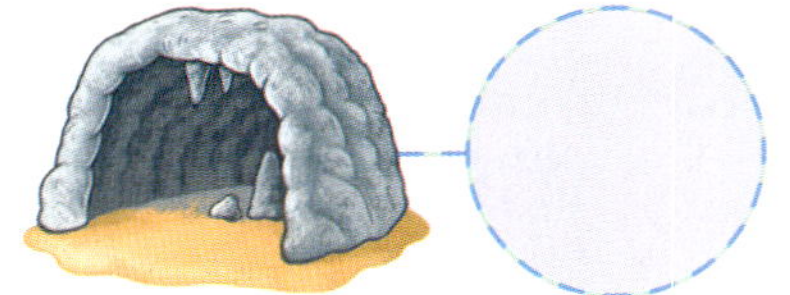 

isten and circle the correct word. Track 05

1. cave	2. feet	3. pine
wave	pie	fine
take	Pete	dive
4. cane	5. ride	6. kite
cake	five	mice
rake	dive	made

isten. If the picture is correct, write ◯. But if not, write ✕. Track 06

 **Read and choose the correct word. Then write.**

1. We go to the __________ .

2. The ________ is by the cave.

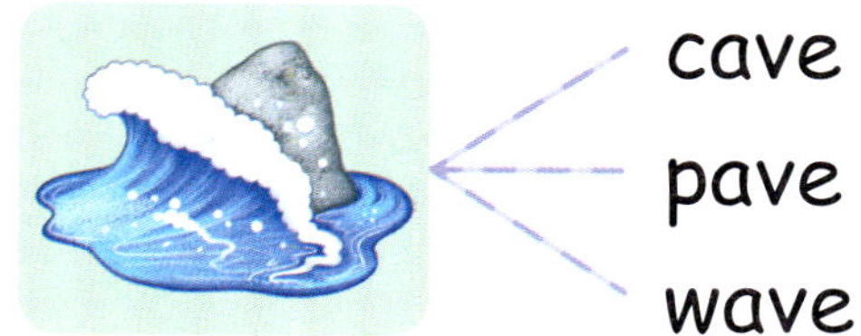

3. He has a ________ .

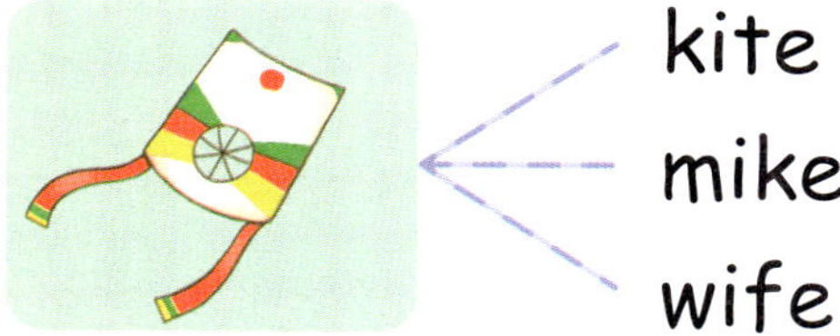

4. The kids have a _________ .

 **Look at the picture and find the correct word.**

m	k	r	a
t	i	a	k
p	a	c	v
b	h	i	e

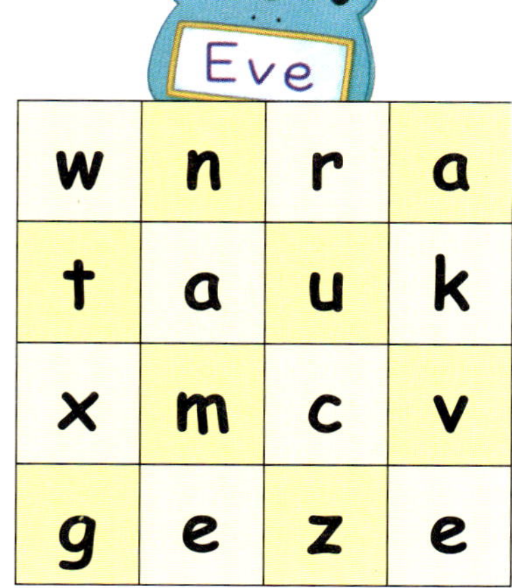

w	n	r	a
t	a	u	k
x	m	c	v
g	e	z	e

m	b	w	u
t	i	a	k
r	i	d	e
n	f	a	t

Read the sentences and choose the correct word.

1. Pet / Pete has a kite.

2. Eve lost a skat / skate .

3. There are five / fiv mice.

In Weird Space!

❶ 주사위를 던지고 이동하면서 단어들을 크게 읽습니다.
❷ 출발했던 곳으로 먼저 도착하는 사람이 승리!

Start →

bike		Pete
	lake	
cave		name

wave		cake
	mice	
Eve		skate

Try Again With Bingo!

먼저 자신의 빙고판을 채우고 위의 게임을 다시 합
니다. 게임에서 이동한 곳의 단어를 읽고 아래의
자신의 빙고판 위의 단어를 지웁니다. 먼저 세 줄
을 완성하는 사람이 승리!

Homework Spot

Track 07

1 Listen. If you hear the pair of words that have a same long vowel sound, write ◯. If you hear the pair of words that have a different sound, write ✕.

1 ☐ 2 ☐ 3 ☐ 4 ☐

2 Listen and connect the pictures to the correct long vowel sounds.

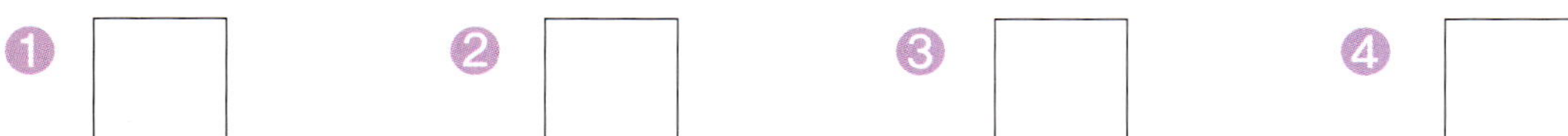

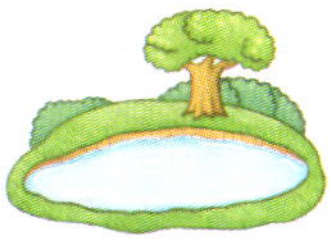

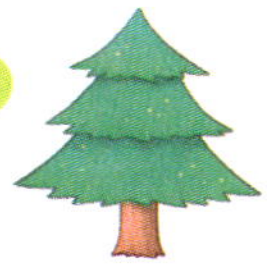

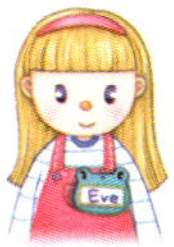

a e i

3 Listen and circle the words that you hear. Then write.

1 There is a ________ near the ________ . (cave / cake / skate / lake)

2 There are ________ ________ . (fire / five / mice / mate)

3 There is a ________ and a ________ . (cake / wave / kite / pine)

4 Look and write the words.

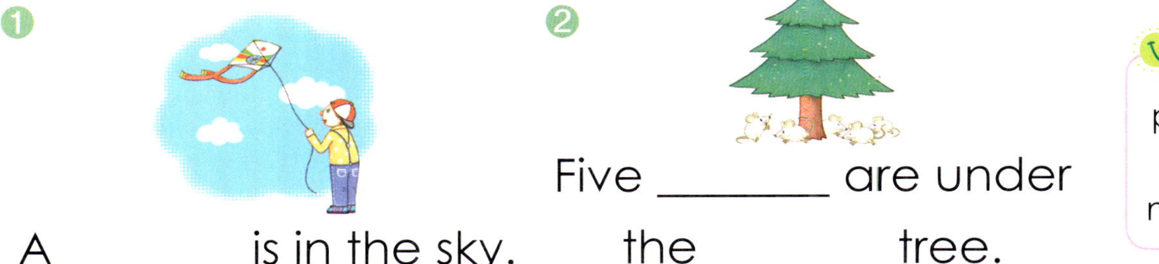

1

A ________ is in the sky.

2

Five ________ are under the ________ tree.

Word Box

pine
kite
mice

Unit 02

Long o, u sound with magic e : o-e, u-e

10min

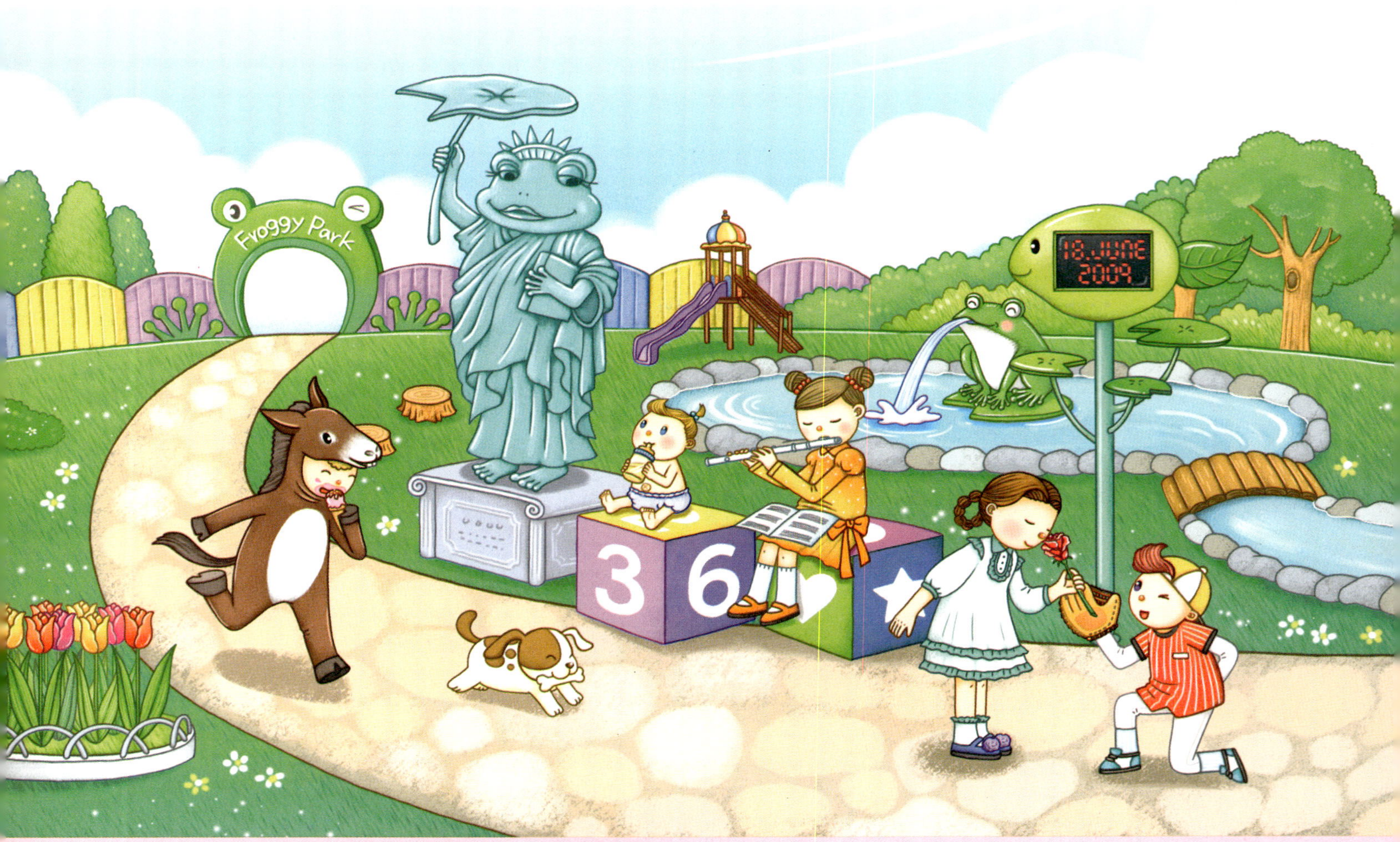

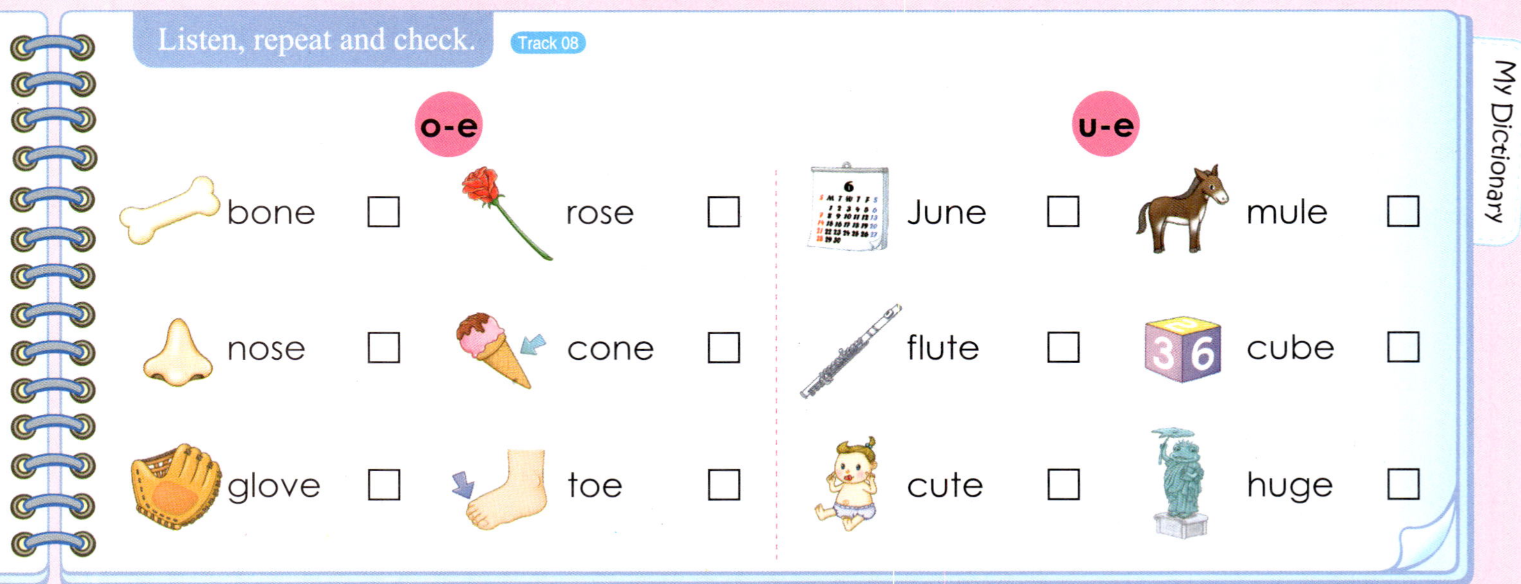

Look and find the new word, then circle.

Listen, repeat and check. Track 08

My Dictionary

o-e

 bone ☐
 rose ☐
 nose ☐
 cone ☐
 glove ☐
 toe ☐

u-e

 June ☐
 mule ☐
 flute ☐
 cube ☐
 cute ☐
 huge ☐

An Odd Poem

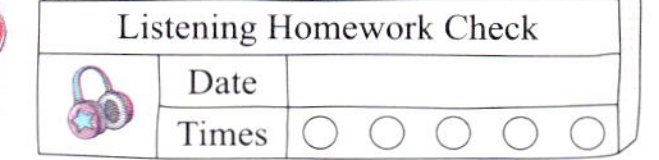

A rose  in the glove

Near by a girl's nose .

A huge  frog looks at

A cute  baby on the cube 3 6.

A mule  eats a cone

Near by huge toes .

Sweet flute sounds meet the ear.

A dog with a **bone** is happy.

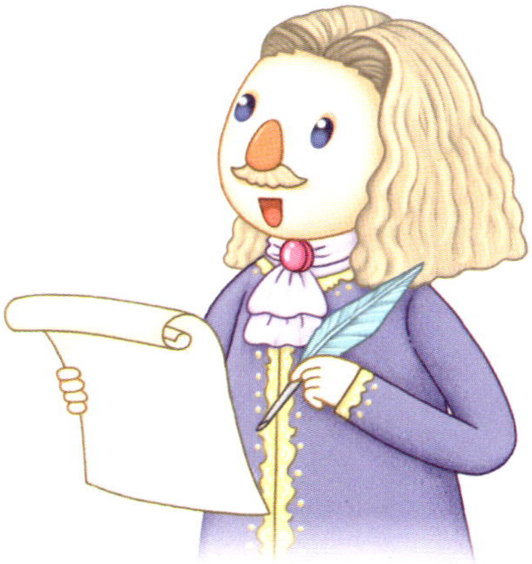

POP QUIZ Look and circle the missing letters.

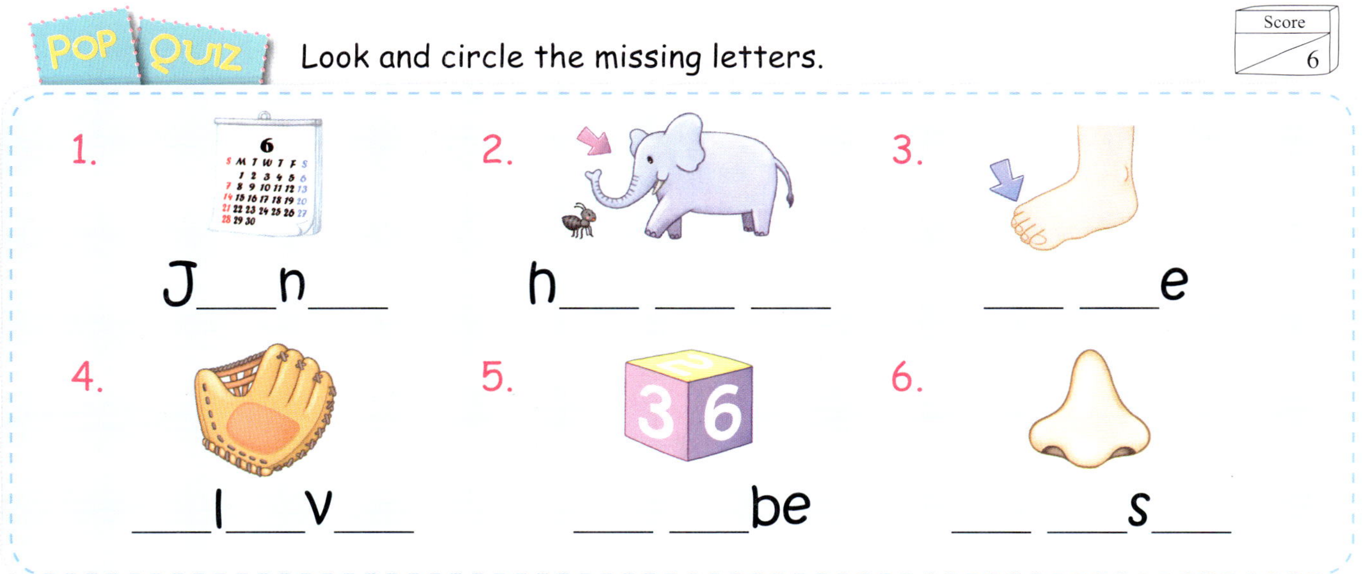

1.   J__n__

2.   h__ __ __

3.   __ __e

4.   __l v__

5.   __ __be

6.   __ __s__

 isten and circle the correct word. **Track 10**

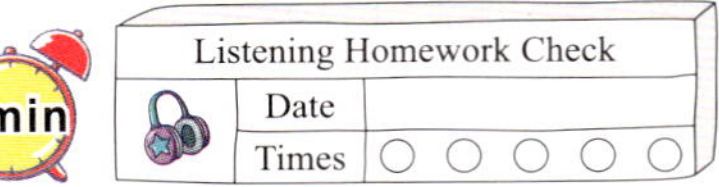

1. two	2. cute	3. joy
toe	cut	job
ten	can	June

4. net	5. huge	6. grow
nose	hug	glue
nut	hut	glove

isten and connect the word to correct long vowel sound. **Track 11**

1. 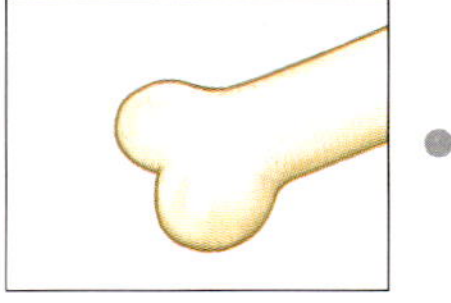

3. 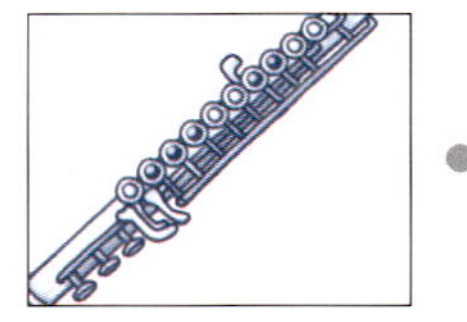

5. 

o

u

2. 

4. 

6. 

isten and number in order. **Track 12**

1. 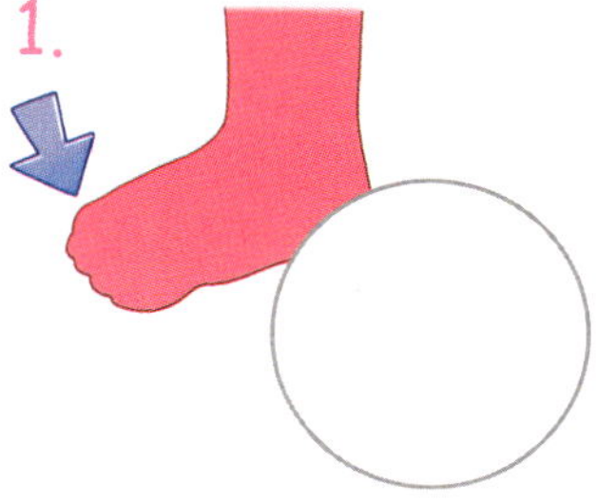

2. 

3. 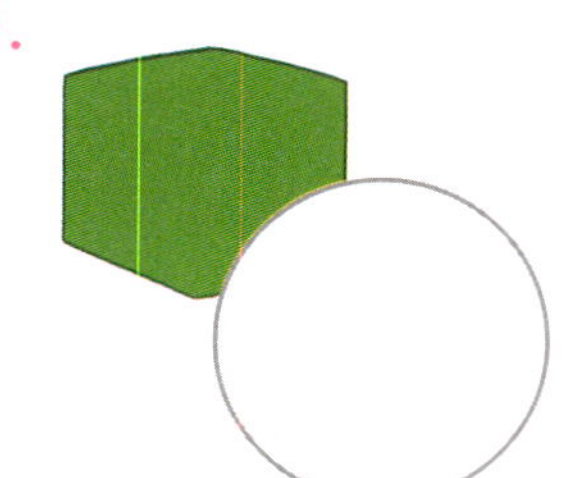

4. 

Color the long vowel **u** words and write the missing letters to complete the word.

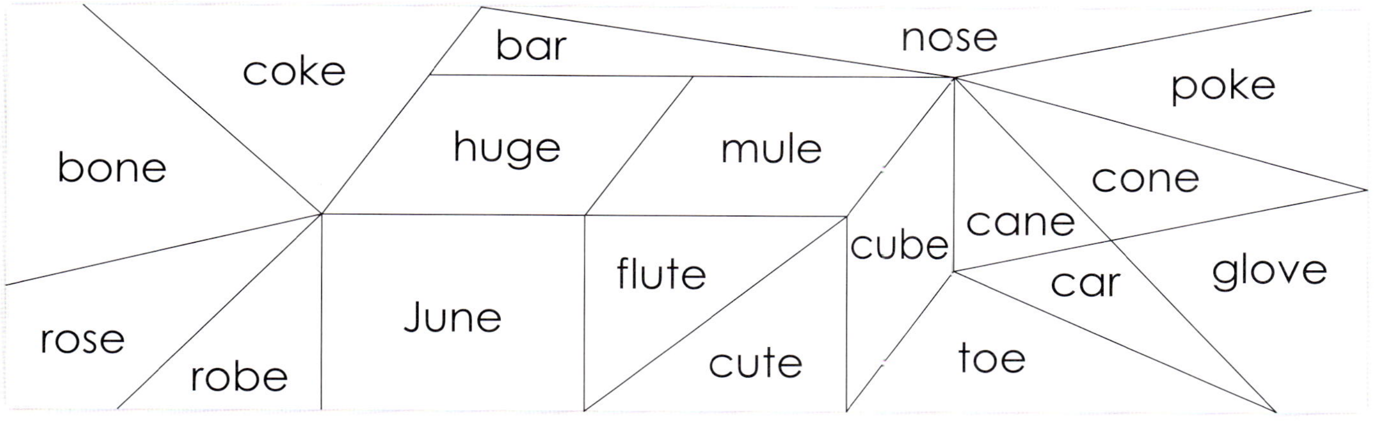

1. h ___ ge   2. J ___ n ___   3. fl ___ te

4. c ___ ___ e   5. m ___ le   6. c ___ t ___

C Check the correct word.

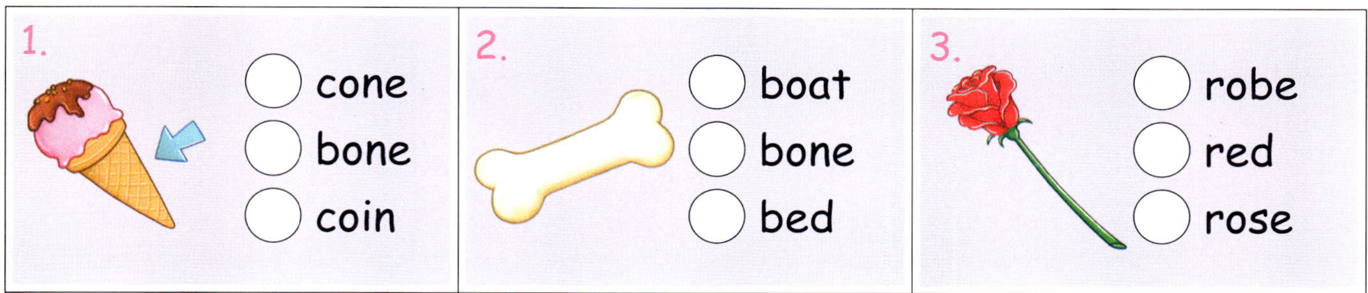

1. ◯ cone ◯ bone ◯ coin

2. ◯ boat ◯ bone ◯ bed

3. ◯ robe ◯ red ◯ rose

MINI TEST Read and choose the words by the pictures.

1. This month is Jude / June .

2. A cut / cute girl has a flute / pluto .

3. A mule / mul eats a corn / cone .

4. A bon / bone is in the grab / glove .

Go Fish!

How to play

❶ 차례를 정하고 자신의 차례에 연못 안에 있는 단어를 찾아서 물고기와 연결합니다.
  그리고 자신의 단어 카드에 그 단어를 씁니다.
❷ 단어를 찾는 동안 다른 플레이어들은 다같이 "1, 2, 3, 4, 5!" 5초를 천천히 셉니다.
❸ 먼저 My Word Box를 다 채우는 사람이 승리!

MY Word Box

Track 13

1 Listen and check the correct picture.

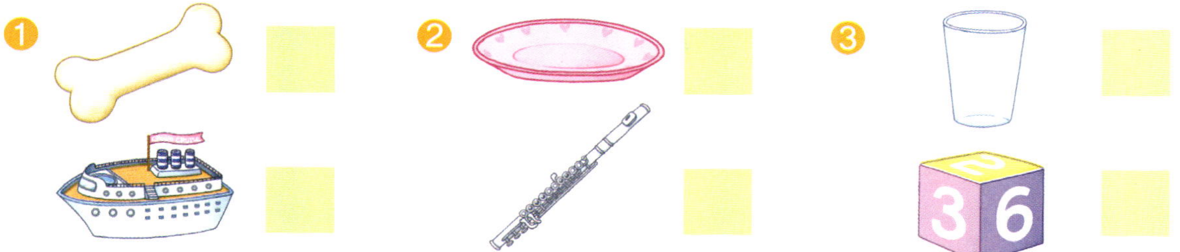

2 Listen and draw a line to the correct word.

3 Listen and circle the correct long vowel sound.

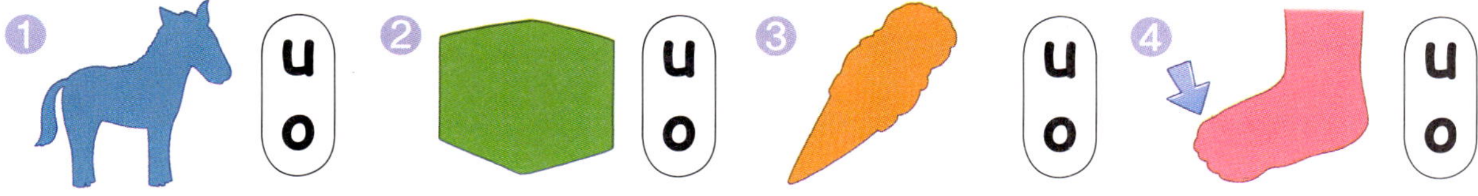

4 Look and write the words.

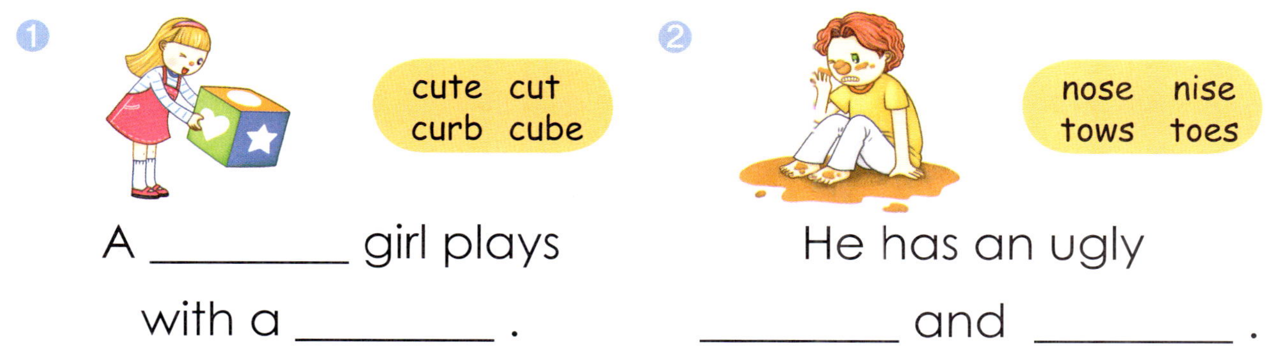

A _________ girl plays

with a _________ .

He has an ugly

_________ and _________ .

Unit 03

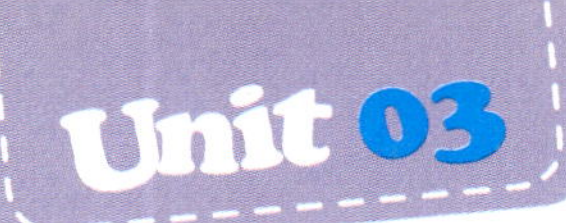

Long a sound with i, y : -ai, -ay

10min

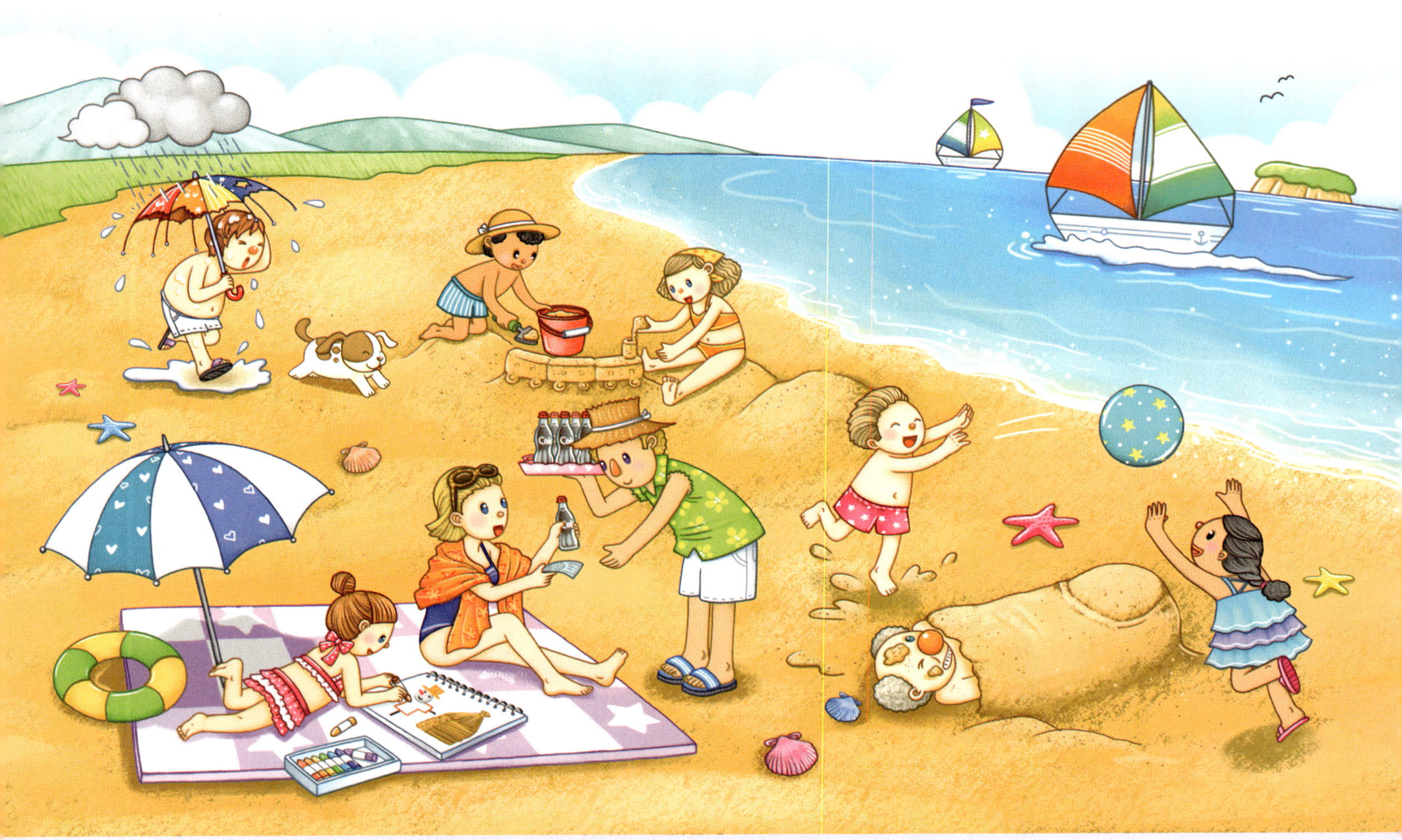

Look and find the new word, then circle.

Listen, repeat and check.

Track 14

My Dictionary

ay						ai					
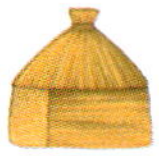	hay	☐	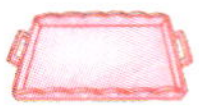	tray	☐	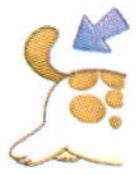	tail	☐	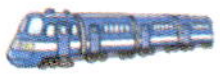	train	☐
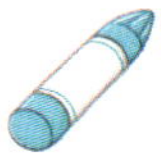	crayon	☐	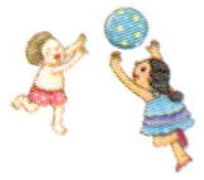	play	☐	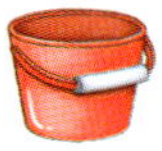	pail	☐	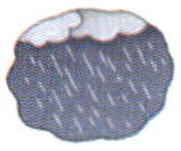	rain	☐
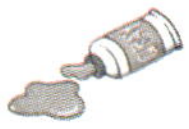	gray	☐	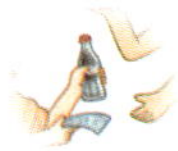	pay	☐	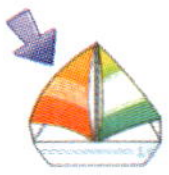	sail	☐	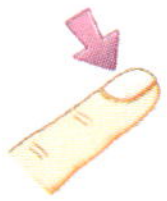	nail	☐

Sing a Joyful Song! Track 15

Verse 1

A and i join together.

A and i make the long /a/ sound.

A and i, ai. A and i, ai.

Ai, ai, ai, in rain! Ai, ai, ai, in train!

Ai, ai, ai, in pail! Ai, ai, ai, in nail!

In sail,sail, sail! In tail, tail, tail!

Rain, train, pail, nail, sail, and tail.

They are ai family.

They are ai family.

Verse 2

A and y join together.

A and y make the long /a/ sound.

A and y, ay. A and y, ay.

Ay, ay, ay, in pay!

Ay, ay, ay, in play!

Ay, ay, ay, in crayon!

Ay, ay, ay in hay!

In gray, gray, gray!

In tray, tray, tray!

Pay, play crayon, hay, gray, and tray!

They are ay family.

They are ay family.

POP QUIZ Listen, and follow the words through the maze. Track 16

Score 6

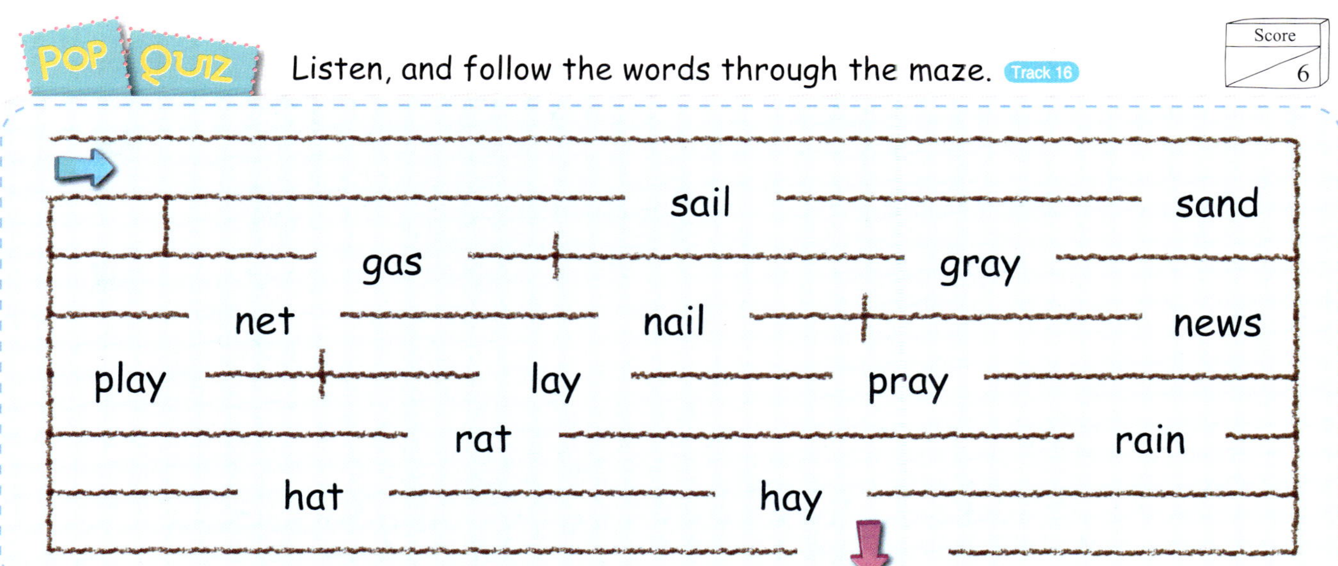

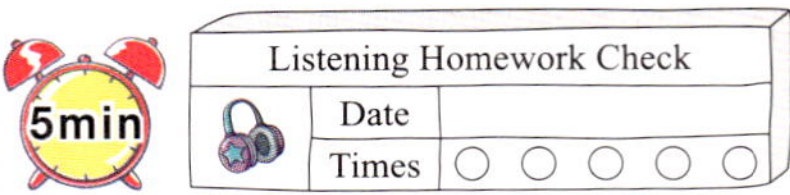

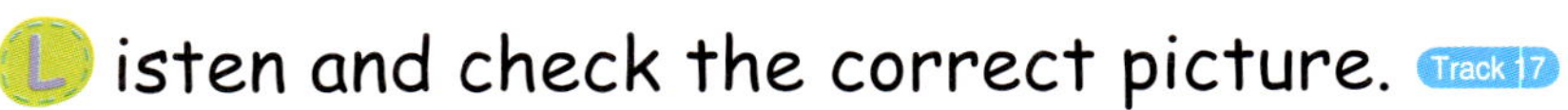 **L**isten and check the correct picture. Track 17

1.  

2.  

3.  

4.  

Listen and draw a line to the correct long vowel sound. Then write. Track 18

1. p___ ___l

2. gr___ ___

3. pl___ ___

4. r___ ___n

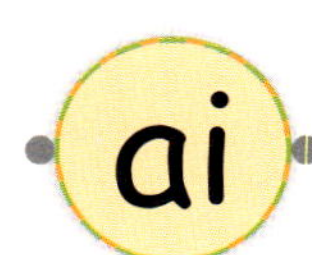

5. t___ ___l

6. cr___ ___on

Listen and choose the correct word. Track 19

1. pie	2. net	3. tray	4. say
pay	rail	tan	sand
pet	nail	tin	sail

Read the name of each picture below. Then write each word in the **5min** correct group.

Long **ay** sound	Long **ai** sound

Word Box
train
tray
sail
hay
nail
crayon

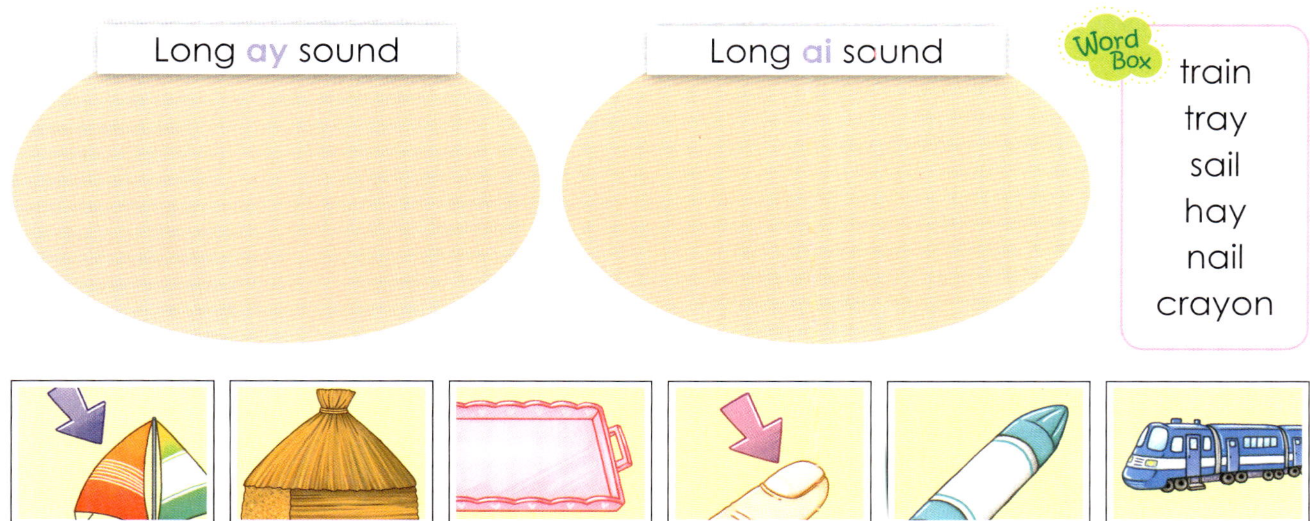

Read and circle all the long **ay** words.

sail	plan	pay	mail	tray
rain	play	ruin	gray	main

Read and circle all the long **ai** words.

train	play	crayon	tail	clay
sail	hay	May	day	rain

MINI TEST Write the long ay or the long ai word in each blank correctly.

1. He colors a __________ gray.

2. My dog has a short __________ .

3. We __________ soccer behind the __________ .

Word Box
play
pail
hay
tail

Word Slides!

 15min 

How to play
❶ 둘이서 미끄럼틀을 하나씩 정합니다.
❷ 차례를 정하고 스피너 중앙에 클립을 놓고 연필로 고정하여 클립을 손가락으로 튕깁니다.
   클립을 돌려서 나온 철자가 자신의 미끄럼틀에 있는 빈칸에 맞으면 써 넣고 그렇지 않으면
   차례를 넘깁니다.
❸ 먼저 미끄럼틀의 빈칸을 다 채우는 사람이 승리!

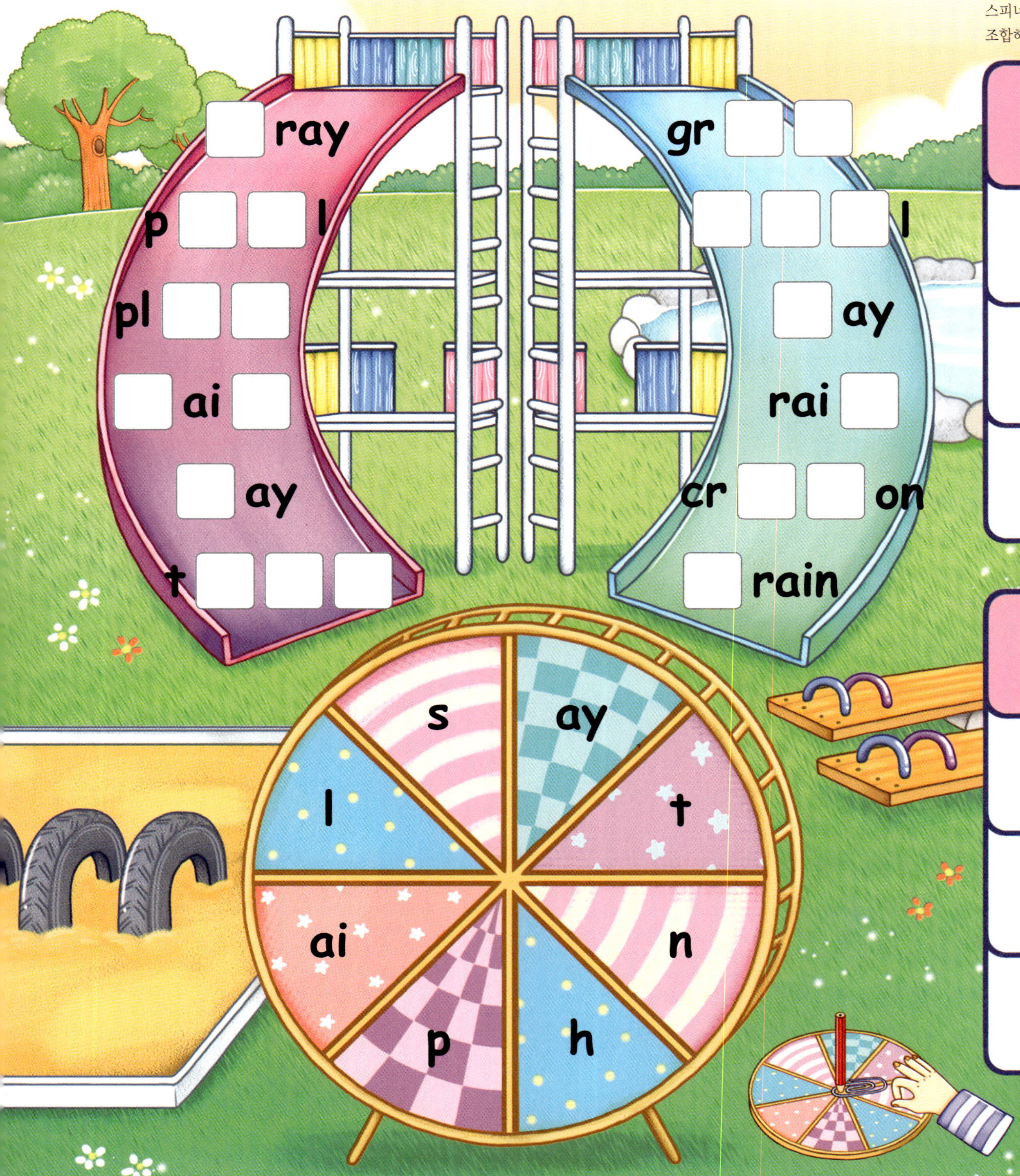

Try Again Word Tag!
스피너를 이용하여 3개의 단어를
조합해서 만들어 보세요.

20

1 Listen. If the picture is correct, write ◯ . But if not, write ✕ .

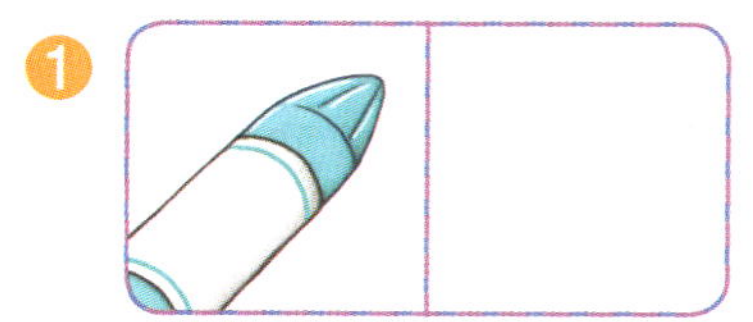  

2 Listen and write the missing letters.

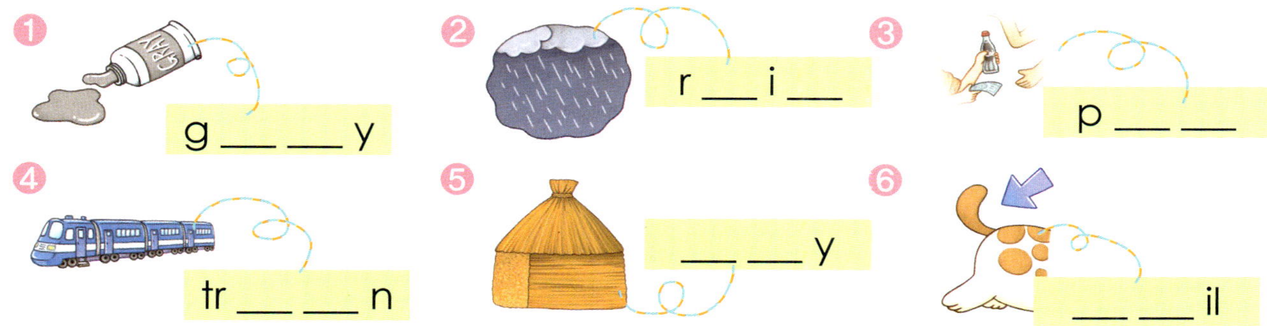

3 Listen and look at the picture. Then choose Yes or No.

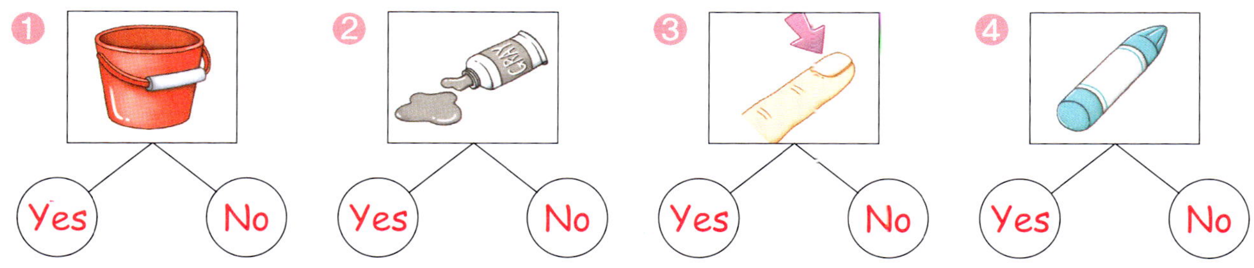

4 Look and complete the sentences.

The goat hides behind the ______ .

The rabbit has a small ______ .

Long **e** sound with **e, a : ee, ea**

10min

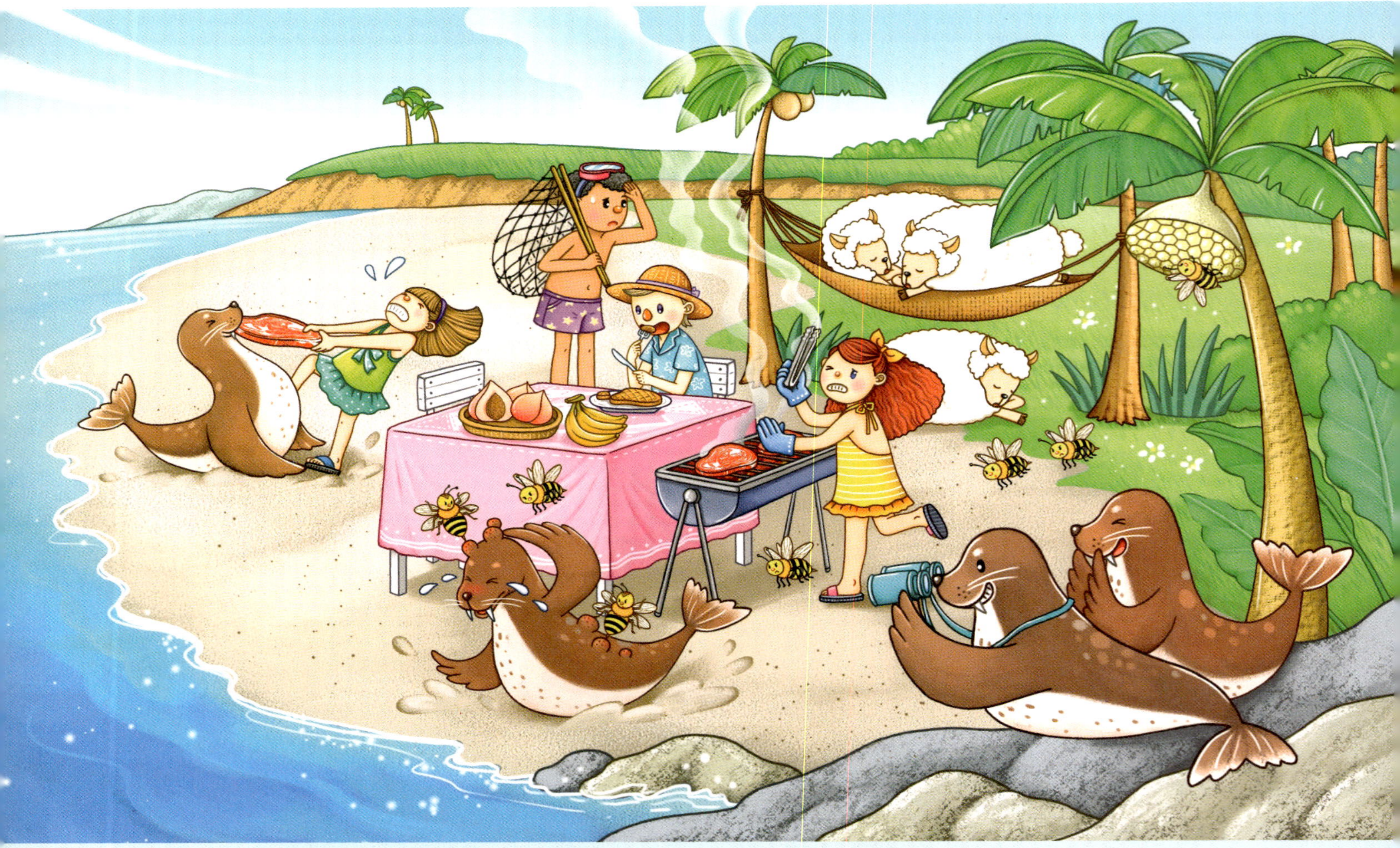

Look and find the new word, then circle.

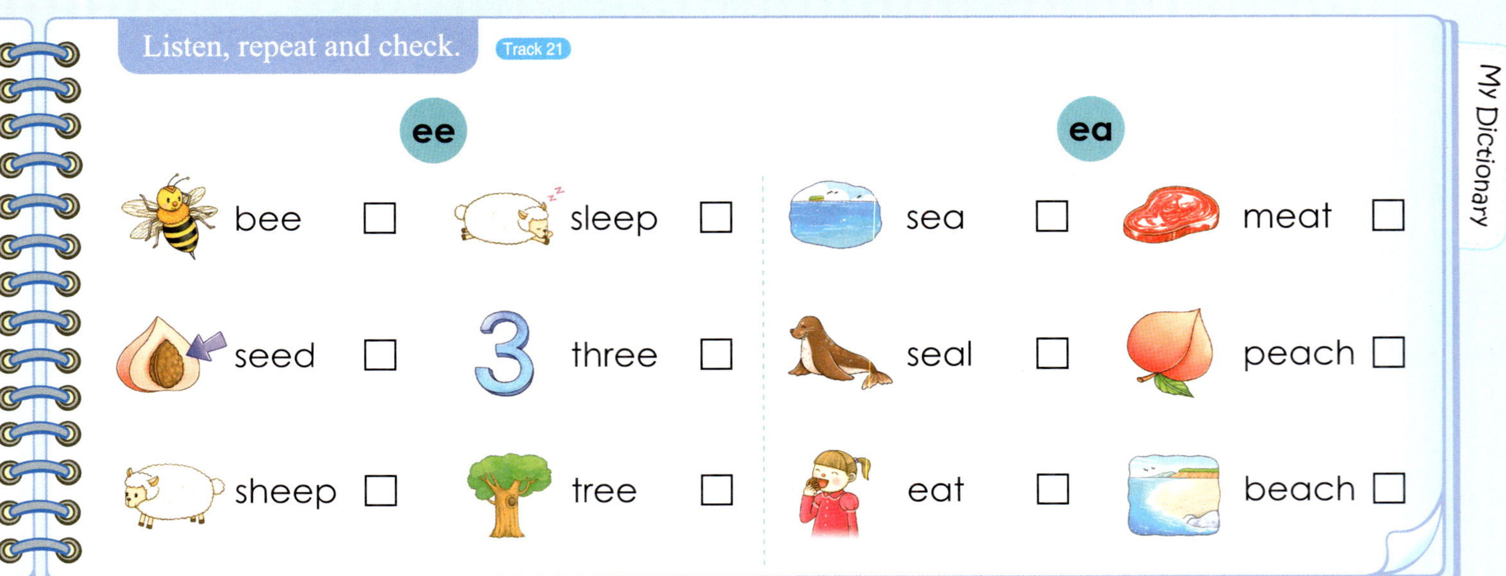

Go for a Jolly Chant!

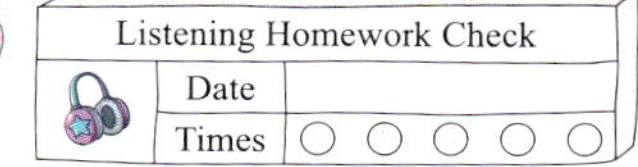

E and e make the long~~/ee/ sound!

Long /ee/ sound in bee and seed.

Long /ee/ sound in sheep and sleep.

Long /ee/ sound in three and tree.

E and e make the long~~/ee/ sound!

E and a make the long~~/ea/ sound!

Long /ea/ sound in sea and seal.

Long /ea/ sound in eat and meat.

Long /ea/ sound in peach and beach.

E and a make the long~~/ea/ sound!

POP QUIZ Listen, and circle the correct long vowel sound.

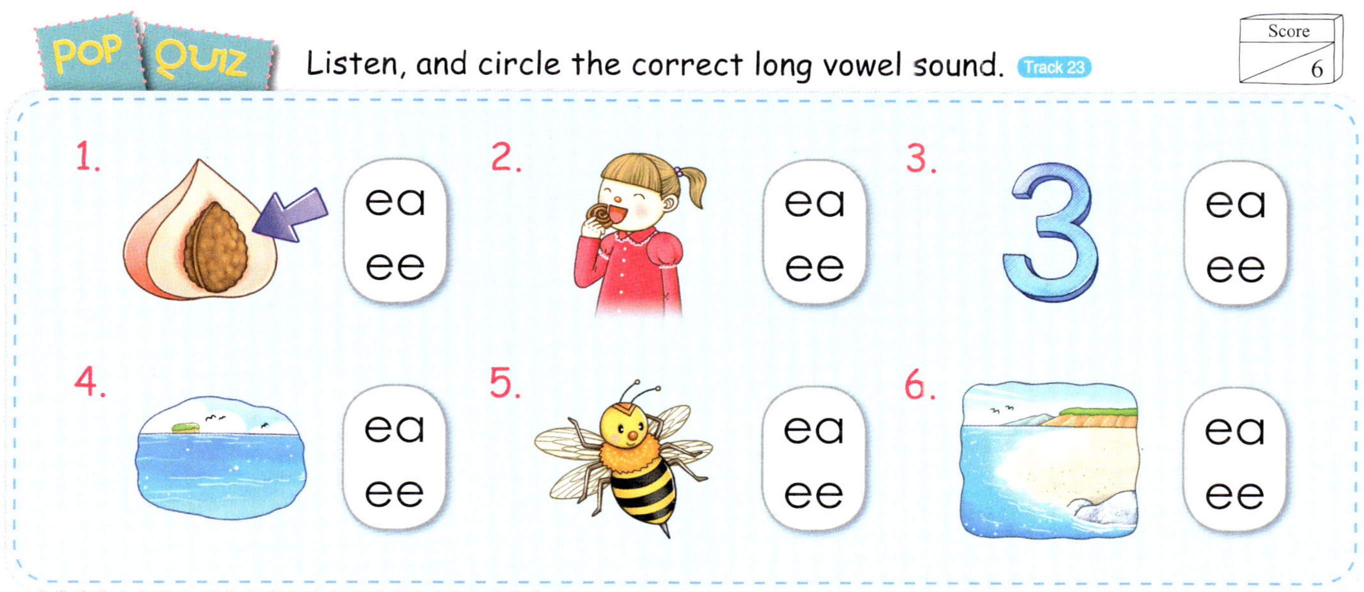

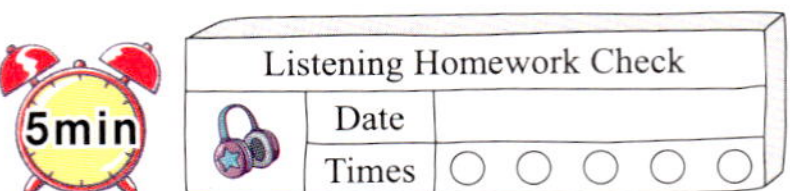

Listen and circle the correct picture. Track 24

1. 2.

3. 4.

Listen and circle the correct picture. Track 25

1. 

2.  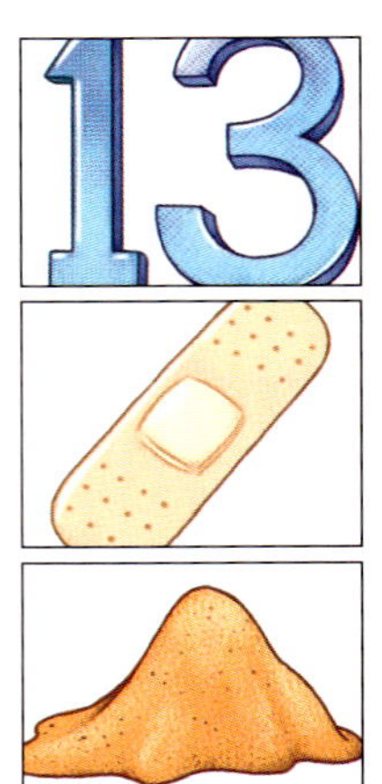 

3. 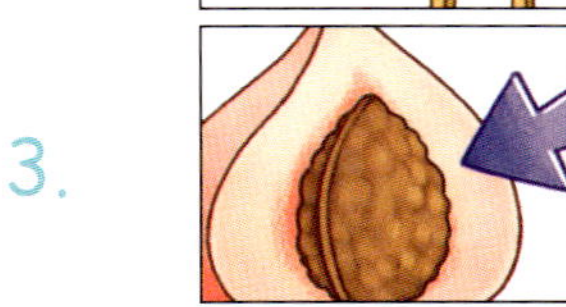

Listen and choose the correct picture. Track 26

1.  2.  3. 

   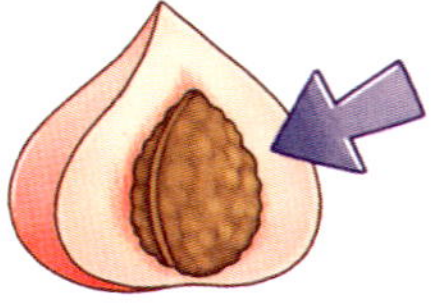

Look at the given word. Make the word, then write.

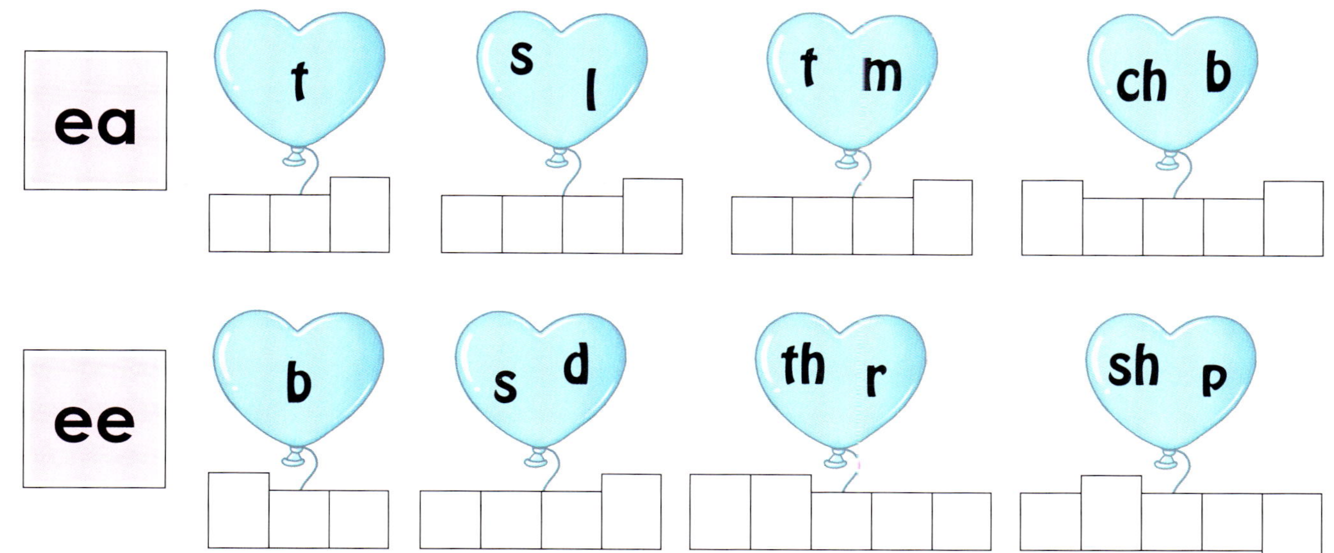

Read the words and choose the correct one.

1. made ○
   meat ○
   mat ○

2. tray ○
   tried ○
   tree ○

3. sheep ○
   shape ○
   spade ○

4. beat ○
   bee ○
   bear ○

5. see ○
   seed ○
   sea ○

6. eat ○
   it ○
   year ○

MINI TEST Read and write the number of the word in the blank.

1. Two seals [ ] on the rock.

2. The dogs [ ] meat.

3. There are [ ] [ ] s.

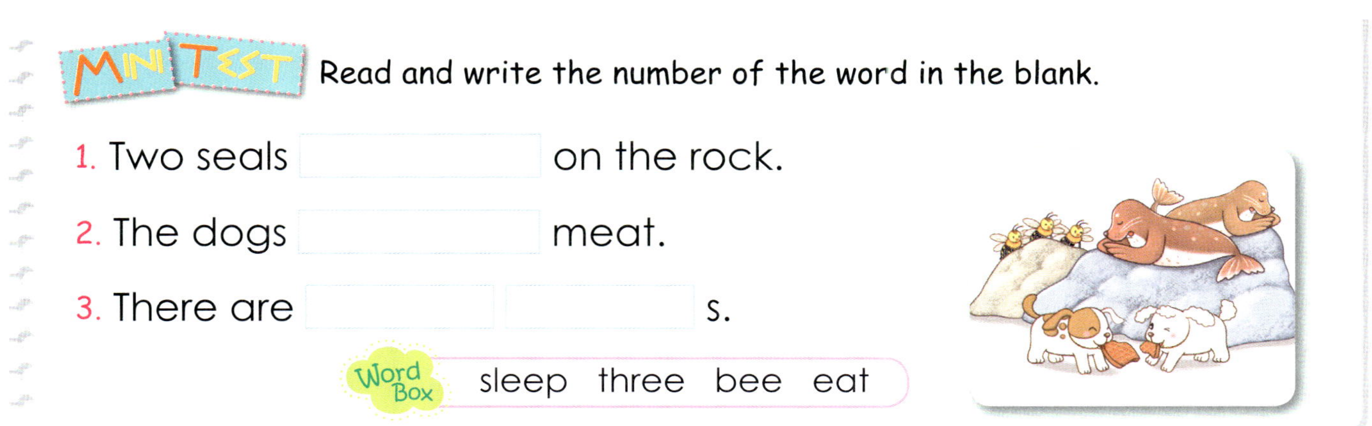

Word Box   sleep   three   bee   eat

Let's Play
Coin Soccer!
15min
a coin   a pencil
3 pts
2 pts
three
2 pts
peach
1 pt
seed
1 pt
sea
1 pt
eat
1 pt
bee
1 pt
sheep
1 pt
seal
1 pt
meat
1 pt
tree
2 pts
beach
2 pts
sleep
3 pts
Ball Card
Long EA vowel words
Long EE vowel words
How to play
❶ 동전을 손가락으로 튕겨서 만난 단어들을 크게 읽습니다. 그리고 아래의 'Ball Card'에 그 단어를 써서 카드를 채웁니다.
❷ 자신이 만난 단어를 읽고 카드에 쓰면 그 단어의 점수를 얻습니다. 또 상대의 골대에 동전을 넣어도 3points 점수를 얻습니다.(골대를 동전이 지나치면 안되고 골대 안에 동전이 걸쳐 있어야 함.)
❸ Ball Card를 다 채우면 게임을 끝내고 점수를 계산합니다. 가장 높은 점수를 얻은 사람이 승리!
Score Board

1 Listen and connect the picture with the sound that you hear.

 1
 2
 3
 4

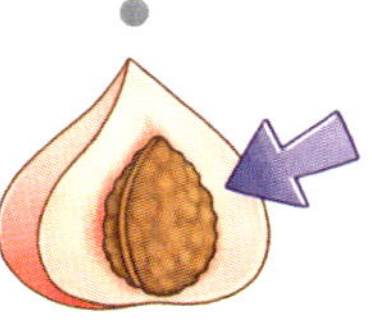

2 Listen and match the common long vowel sound of the two words that you hear.

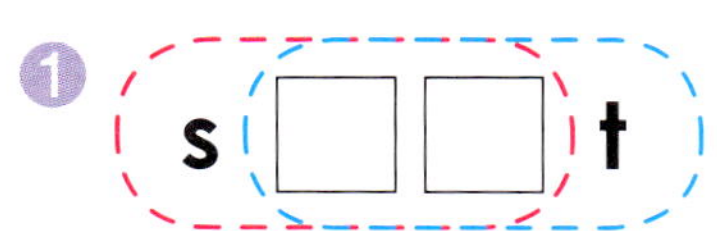
① s □ □ t

ee

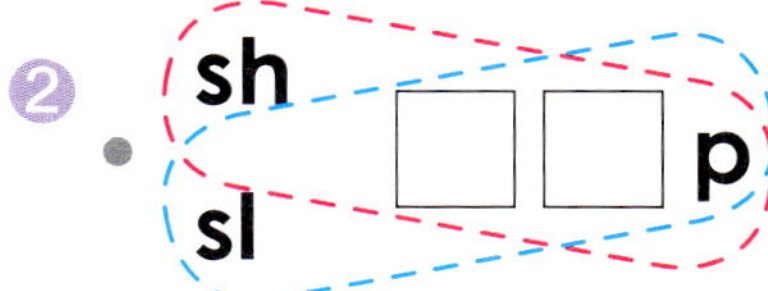
② sh / sl □ □ p

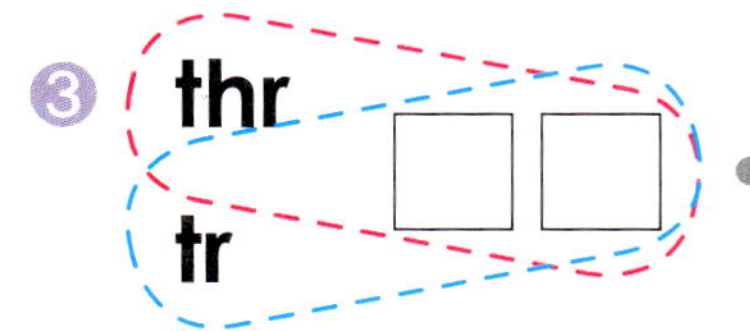
③ thr / tr □ □

ea

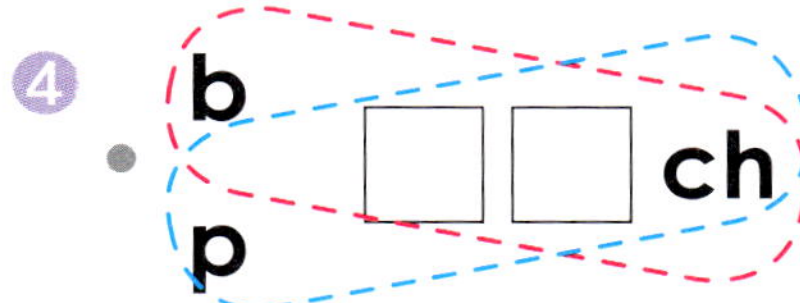
④ b / p □ □ ch

3 Do the crossword.

Long e sound : -ey, -e & Long i sound : -ie, y

Look and find the new word, then circle.

Listen, repeat and check.   Track 28

-ey		-e		-ie		-y	
 key	 ☐	we	 ☐	die	 ☐	spy	☐
 donkey	 ☐	she	 ☐	tie	 ☐	sky	☐
 monkey	 ☐	he	 ☐	lie	 ☐	cry	☐
 turkey	 ☐	me	 ☐	pie	 ☐	fly	☐

Thanksgiving Party!

 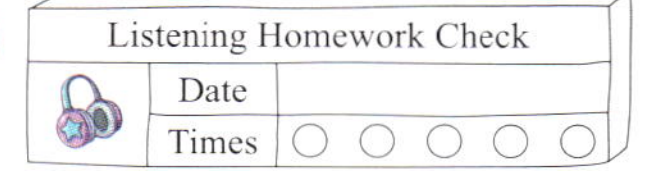

It's Thanksgiving day.

We  spy  a party.

He  wears a tie .

A turkey  and a pie 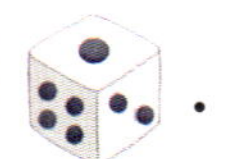 are on the table.

We  play with a die .

A monkey  lies .

A spy  is on the roof.

What is he looking for?

It must be a key.

But...the key is in my hand.

POP QUIZ Listen, and write the missing letters.

1. turk___ ___

2. fl___

3. cr___

4. sh___

5. p___ ___

6. t___ ___

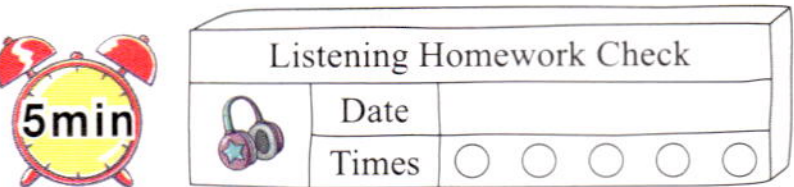

 **L** isten and number in order. Track 31

 **L** isten and circle the correct word. Track 32

1. ski
   sky
   skate

2. pie
   pee
   pea

3. den
   day
   die

4. tea
   tie
   time

5. cry
   clay
   cream

6. flee
   fly
   free

 **L** isten. If the picture is correct, write ◯ . But if not, write ✗ . Track 33

1. 
2. 
3. 
4. 

 **R**ead and choose the correct word and write.

1. A _______ is outside.

- donkey
- monkey
- turkey

2. He wears a _______ .

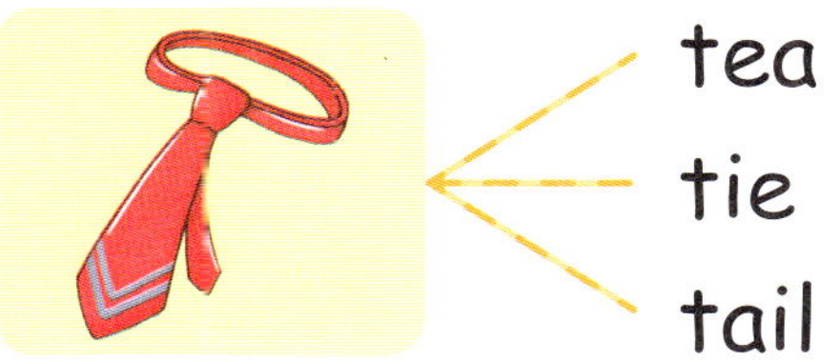

- tea
- tie
- tail

3. The moon is in the night _______ .

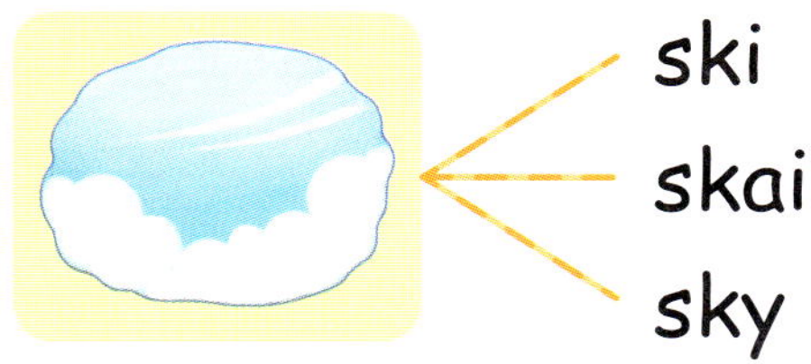

- ski
- skai
- sky

4. _______ is playing a game.

- He
- We
- She

Look at the picture and find the correct word.

n	k	r	a
t	c	a	k
p	q	r	v
b	h	i	y

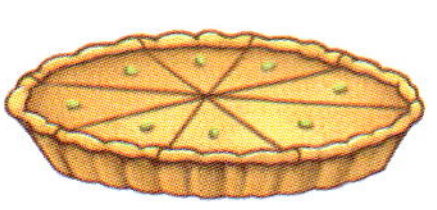

w	p	u	v
t	i	u	k
x	e	b	v
g	r	z	e

m	t	q	o
t	i	a	k
r	f	l	y
z	f	a	t

 **MINI TEST** Read the sentences and choose the correct word.

1. A pei / pie is on the table.

2. He has a day / die .

3. A spi / spy is on the roof.

In a Wild Jungle!

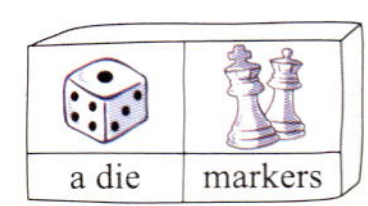

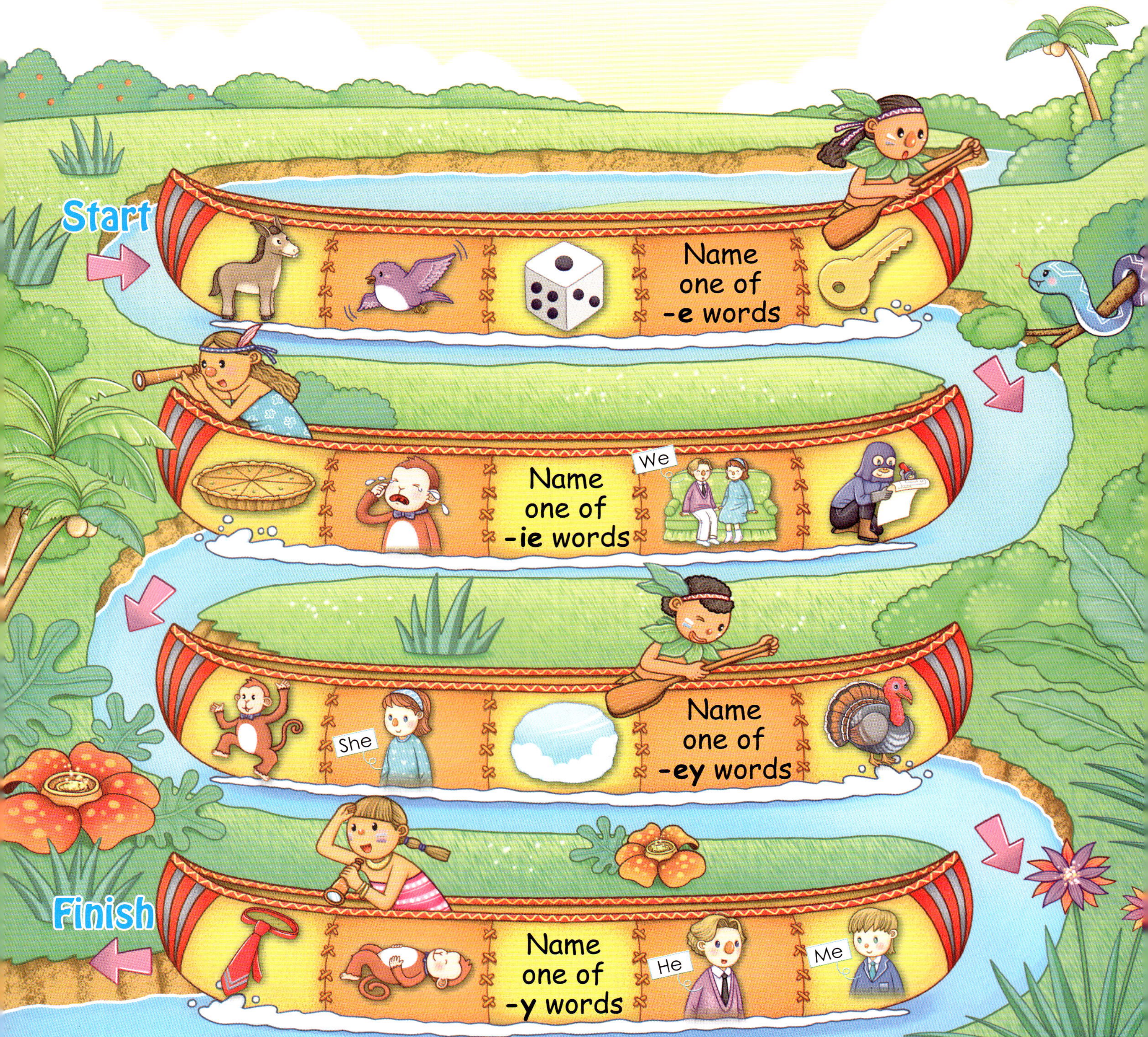

How to play

❶ 주사위를 던지고 이동하면서 그림들을 크게 읽거나 지시어에 따라 단어를 만들어 말하도록 합니다.

❷ 그림들을 못 읽었을 경우, 원래의 위치로 돌아갑니다. (움직일 수 없습니다.)

❸ 출발해서 아래의 끝까지 먼저 도착하는 사람이 승리!

1 Listen. If the word pair has the same long vowel sound, write ◯. But if not, write ✗.

❶ ❷ ❸ ❹

2 Listen and connect the pictures to the correct long vowel sound.

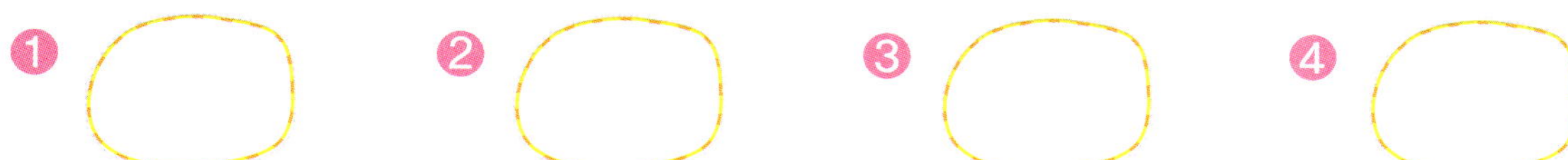

3 Read and choose the two correct words. Then write.

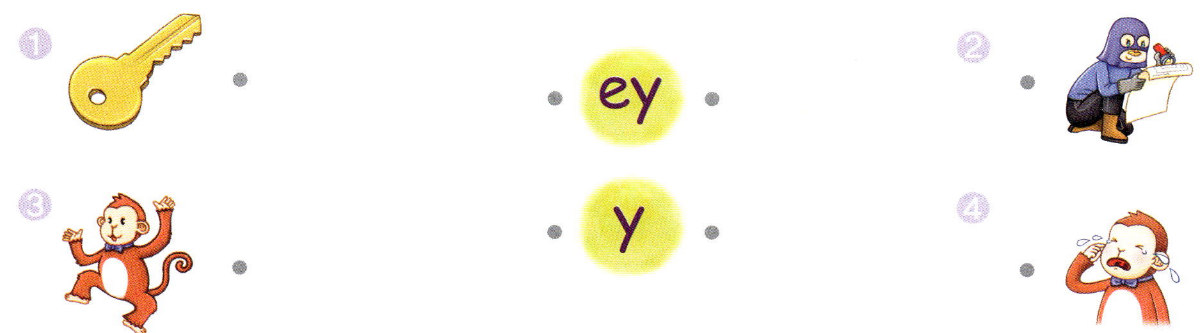

4 Read and write the word to match the picture.

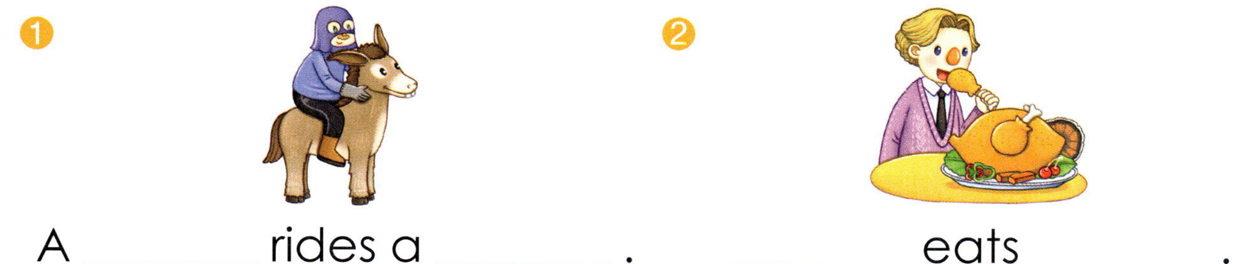

Unit 06

Long o sound with a, e : -oa-, -oe-

10min

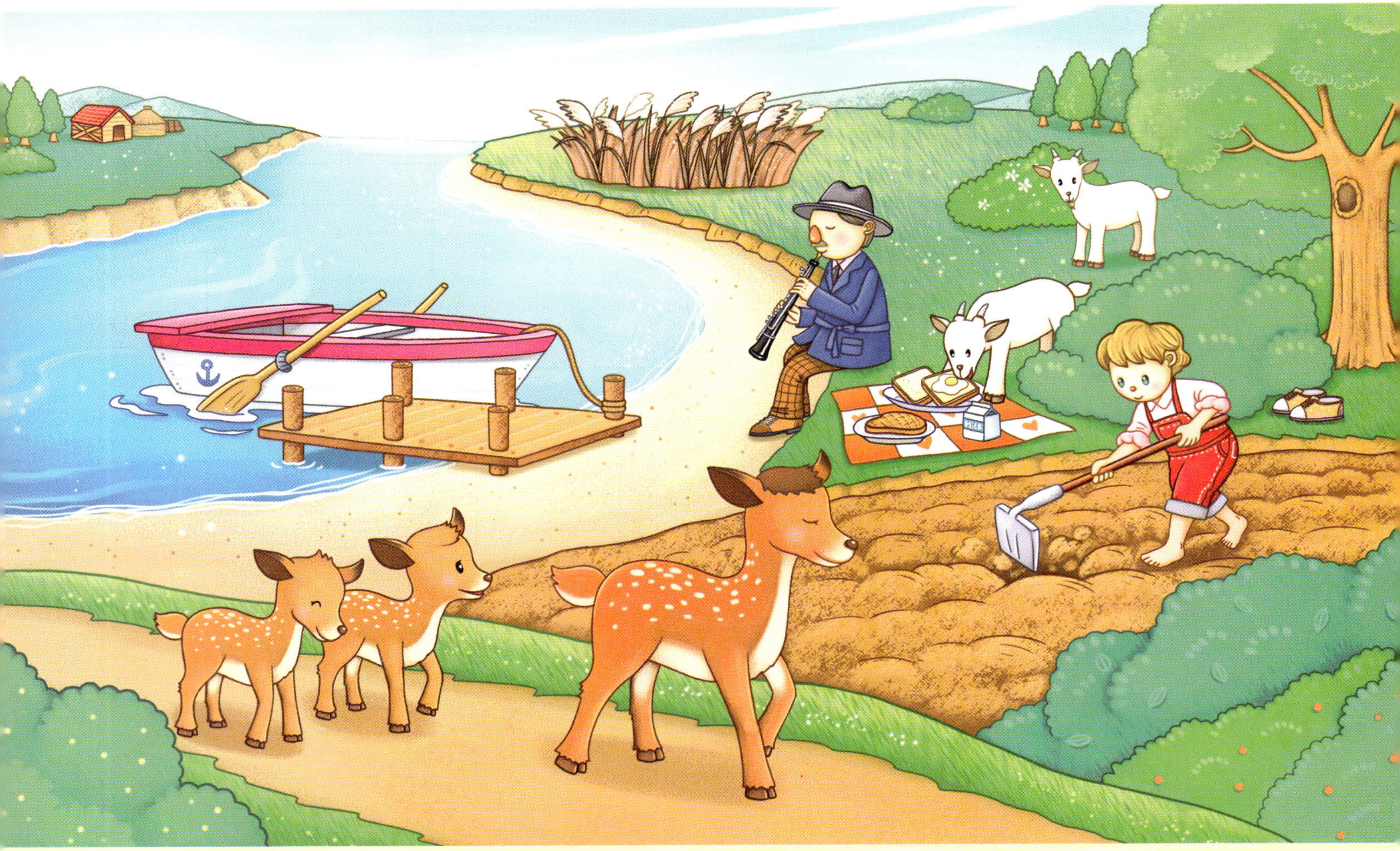

Look and find the new word, then circle.

My Dictionary

Listen, repeat and check. Track 35

-oa				-oe			
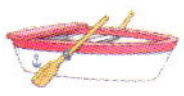	boat	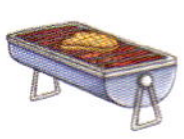	roast	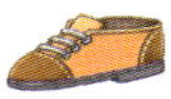	shoe	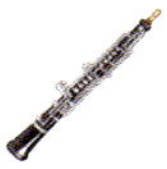	oboe
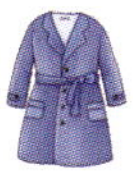	coat	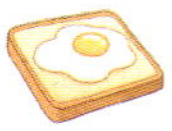	toast	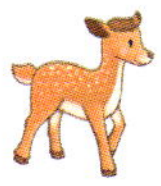	doe	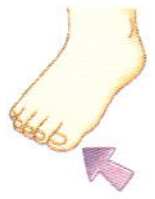	toe
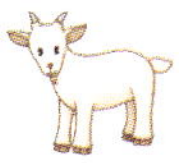	goat	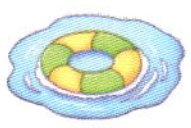	float	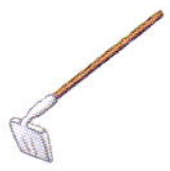	hoe	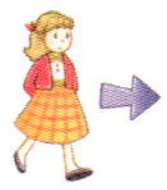	goes

An Odd Poem

A boat  is floating .

An oboe's tune is floating , too.

Toast and roast bee= for a man.

They are not for goats .

Why is a goat eating quietly?

Why doesn't he know it?

A doe goes by a boy.

He is hoeing .

A boy's toes on the field.

Where are his shoes ?

POP QUIZ Listen, and circle the letters to complete the words.

Score 6

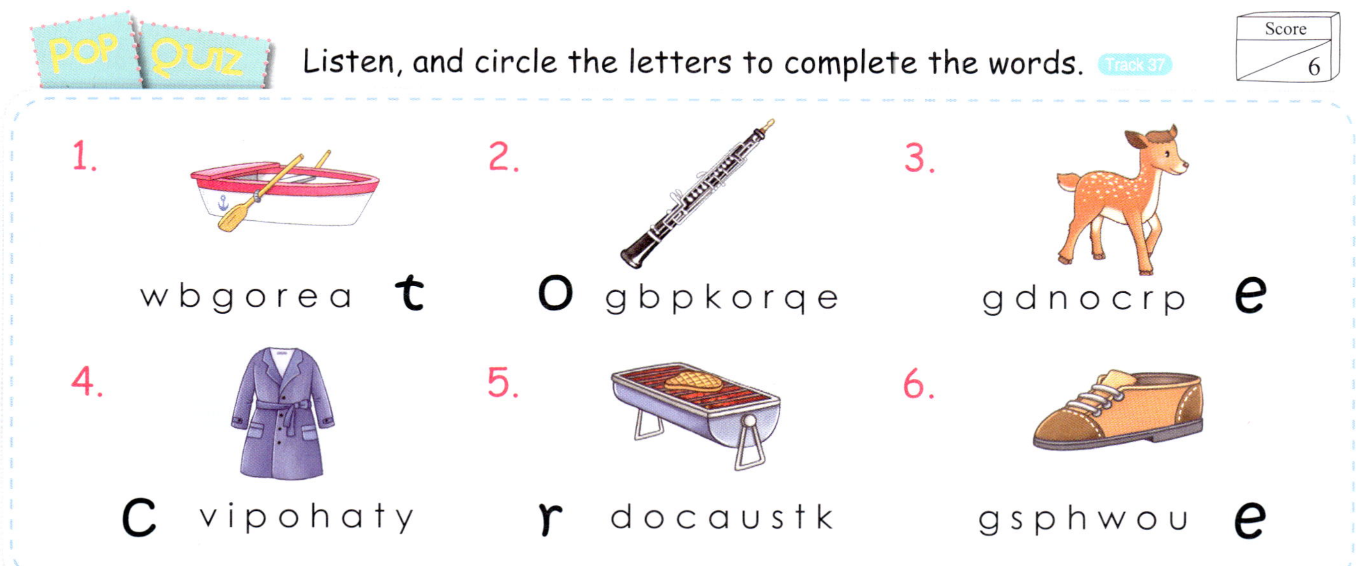

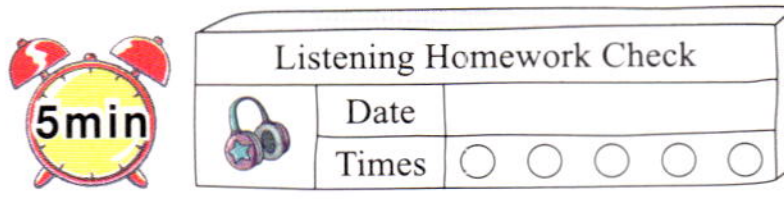

Listen and circle the correct word. Track 38

1. toe
tote
tute

2. goat
got
gate

3. plot
float
flake

4. how
horn
hoe

5. goes
gain
goe

6. test
toast
tone

Listen and connect the word to correct long vowel sound. Track 39

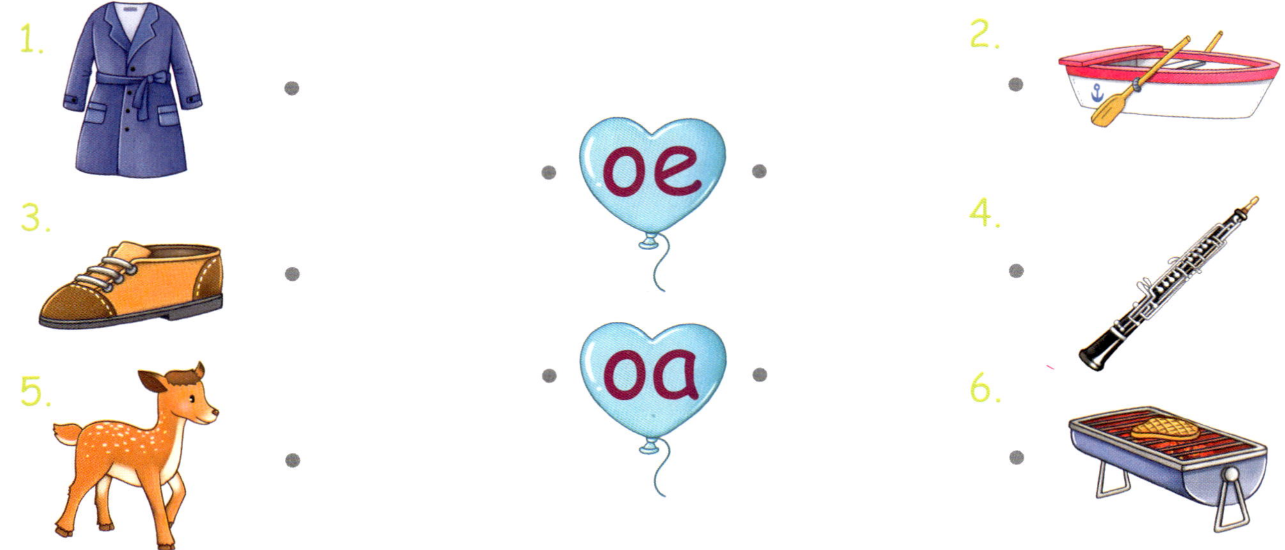

1.
2.
3.
4.
5.
6.

Listen and number in order. Track 40

Color the long vowel **oe** words and write the missing letters to complete the word.

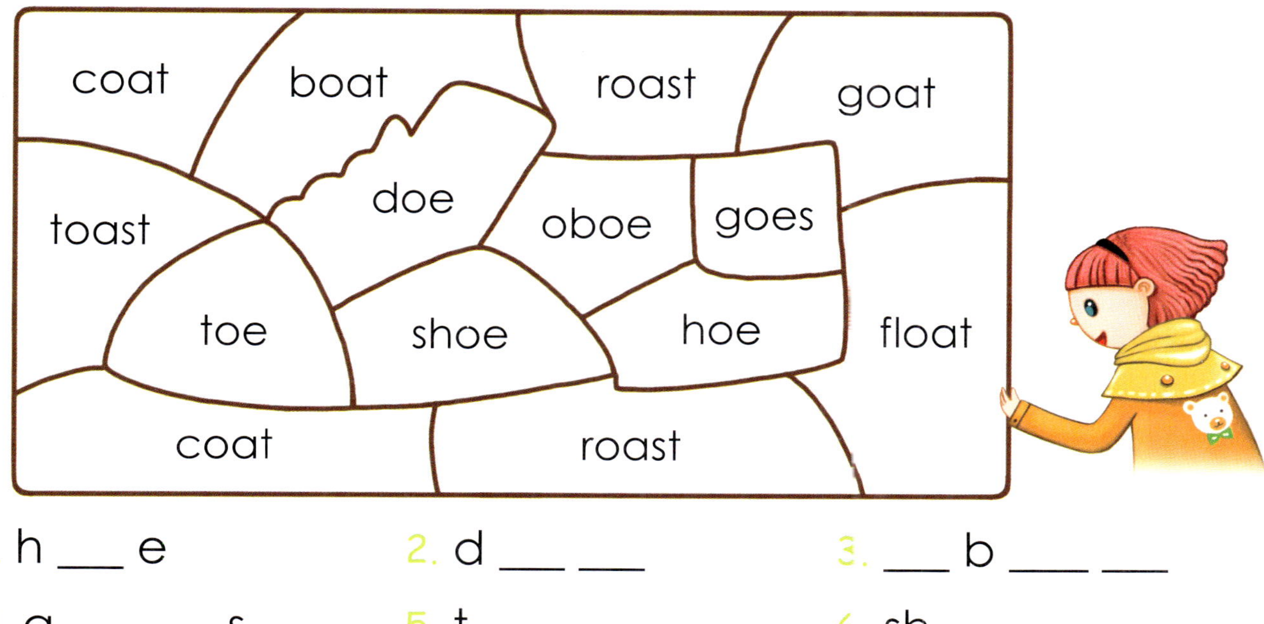

1. h __ e
2. d __ __
3. __ b __ __
4. g __ __ s
5. t __ __
6. sh __ __

Check the correct word.

MINI TEST Read and choose the words.

1. The boat flutes / floats .

2. A man plays the oboe / obey .

3. Two goats / gates eat test / toast .

4. A doe hoes / goes near a man.

Let's Play
Leap Frogs!
15min
How to play
❶ 자신의 차례에 개구리의 단어 퍼즐을 풀면 연못 안 그림의 단어가 나옵니다.
그 단어를 쓰고 개구리와 연결합니다.
❷ 단어 퍼즐을 푸는 동안 다른 플레이어들은 다같이 "1, 2, 3, 4, 5!" 5초를 천천히 셉니다.
❸ 단어를 많이 풀고 그림을 많이 찾는 사람이 승리!
g+load -l+t-d
h+woe-w
hoe
t+roe-r
b+soa -s+t
c+road -r+t-d
d+foe-f
o+b +voe-v
t+foal -f-l+st
r+toad -t+st-d
g+joe -j+s
fl+soap -s+t-p
sh+poe-p
38

1 Listen and check the correct picture.

2 Listen and draw a line to match the picture to the correct word.

3 Listen and circle the letter for its long vowel sound.

4 Listen and choose the correct words, and write them in the blanks.

1 Poe eats some __________ with roast beef.   toast   toad

2 Joe hid his toy boat under his __________ .   coal   coat

Long u sound with i, e : -ui-, -ue

10min

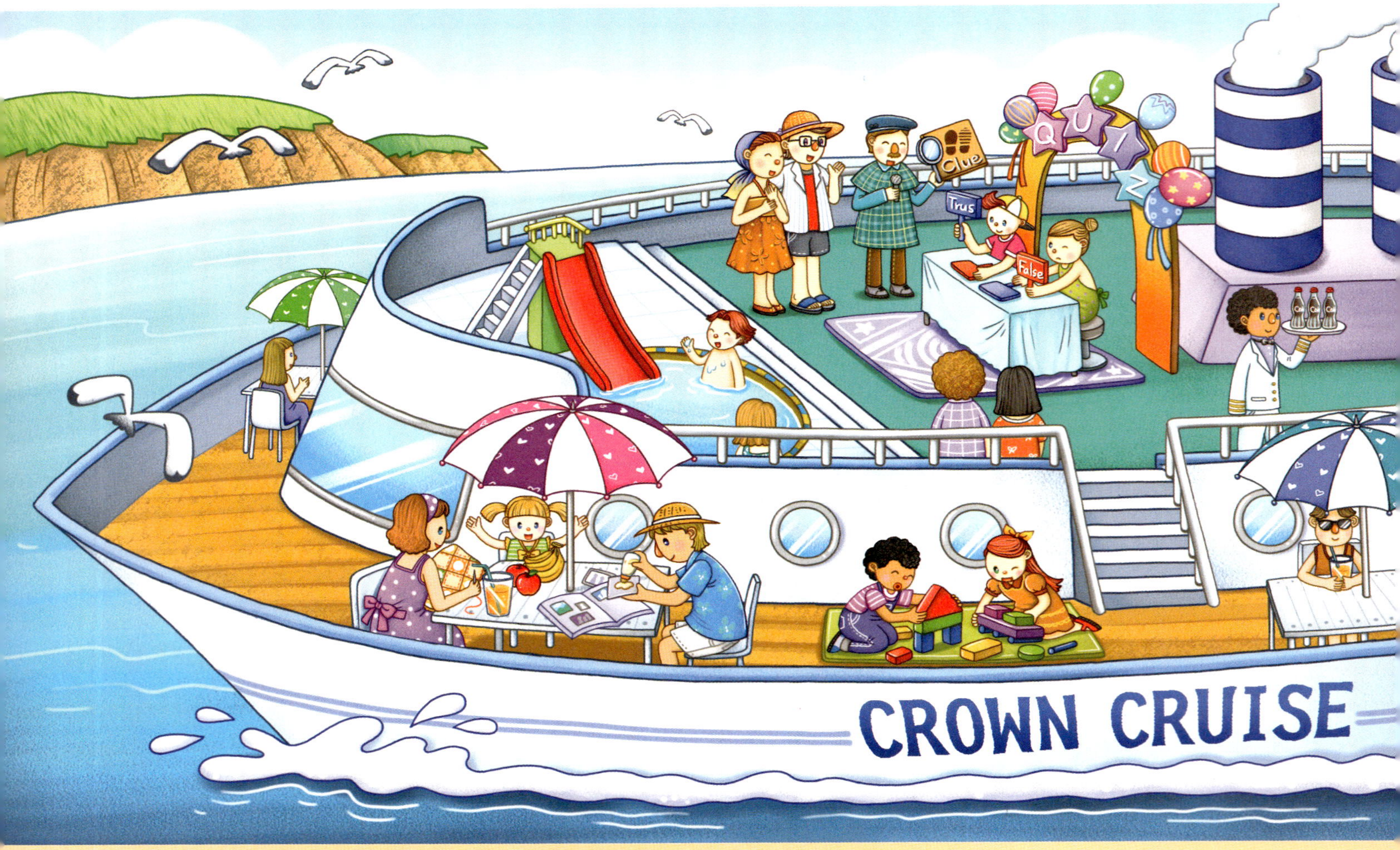

Look and find the new word, then circle.

Listen, repeat and check. | Track 42

-ui

build ☐   suit ☐

fruit ☐   cruise ☐

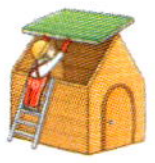

juice ☐   quilt ☐

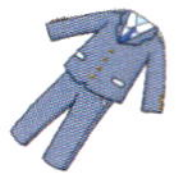

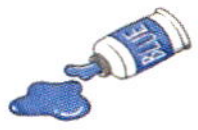

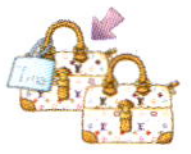

-ue

blue ☐   true ☐

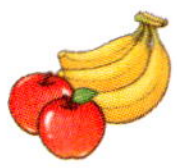

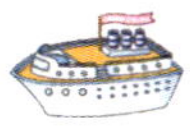

flue ☐   clue ☐

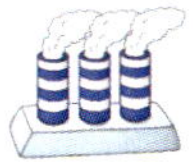

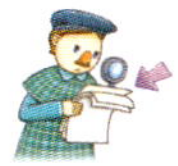

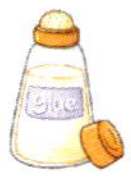

glue ☐   Sue ☐

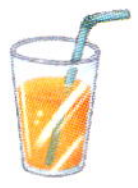

My Dictionary

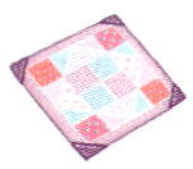

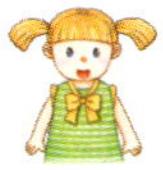

Sing a Joyful Song!  Track 43

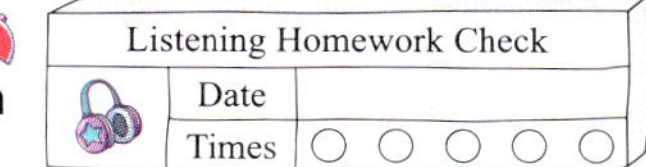

Verse 1

U and i join together.

U and i make the long /ui/ sound.

U and i, /ui/. U and i, /ui/.

Ui, ui, ui in build!

Ui, ui, ui in fruit !

Ui, ui, ui in juice!

Ui, ui, ui in cruise!

In suit, suit, suit!

In quilt, quilt, quilt!

They are ui family.

They are ui family.

Verse 2

U and e join together.

U and e make the long /ue/ sound.

U and e, /ue/. U and e, /ue/.

Ue, ue, ue in blue!

Ue, ue, ue in glue!

Ue, ue, ue in flue!

Ue, ue, ue in clue!

In Sue, Sue, Sue!

In true, true, true!

They are ue family.

They are ue family.

 Listen, and follow the words through the maze. Track 44

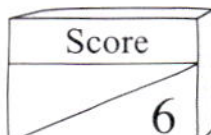

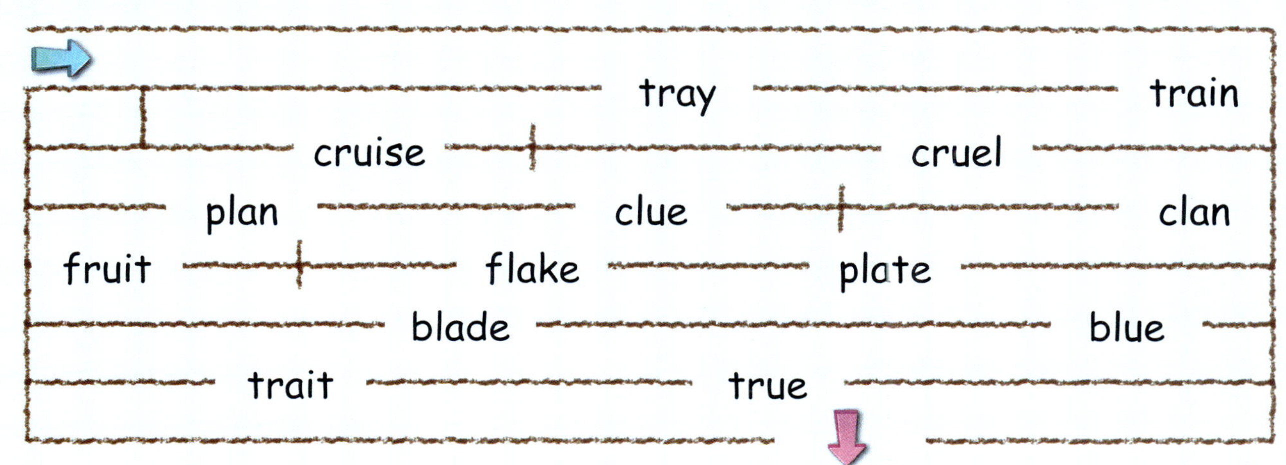

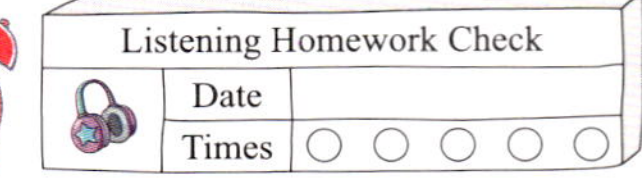

Listen and write ⭕ in the box under the correct picture. `Track 45`

1.  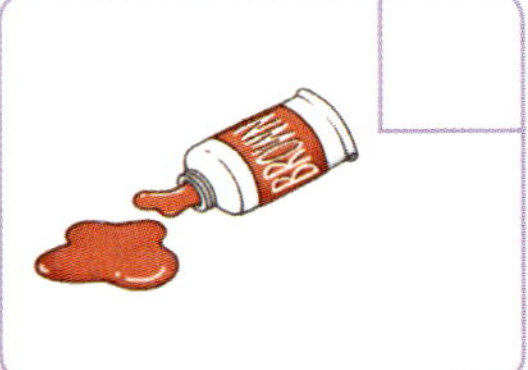

2. 

3.  

4. 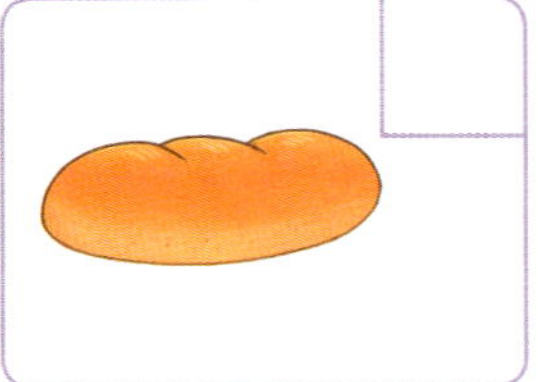

Listen and connect the each word to the correct long vowel sound. `Track 46`

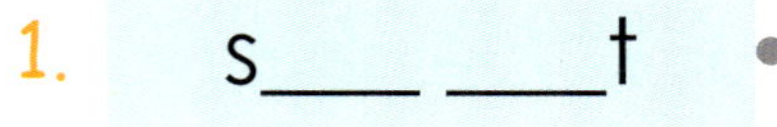

1. s____ ____t

2. cr____ ____se

3. fl____ ____

4. cl____ ____

5. tr____ ____

6. j____ ____ce

Listen and choose the correct word that has the long vowel sound /ui/ or /ue/. `Track 47`

1. build
   bald
   belt

2. blow
   blue
   blind

3. saw
   see
   Sue

4. quail
   quilt
   quarter

Read the name of each picture below. Then write.

Long **ui** sound	Long **ue** sound

Read and circle all the long **ui** words.

bull	build	role	juice	tray
cruise	crown	suit	train	quilt

Read and circle all the long **ue** words.

blue	lush	glue	tall	Sue
rail	true	mole	flue	pole

 Write the long **ui** or the long **ue** word in each blank.

1. A sailor wears a white __________ .

2. My mom makes a __________ .

3. She saw a __________ __________ in the picture.

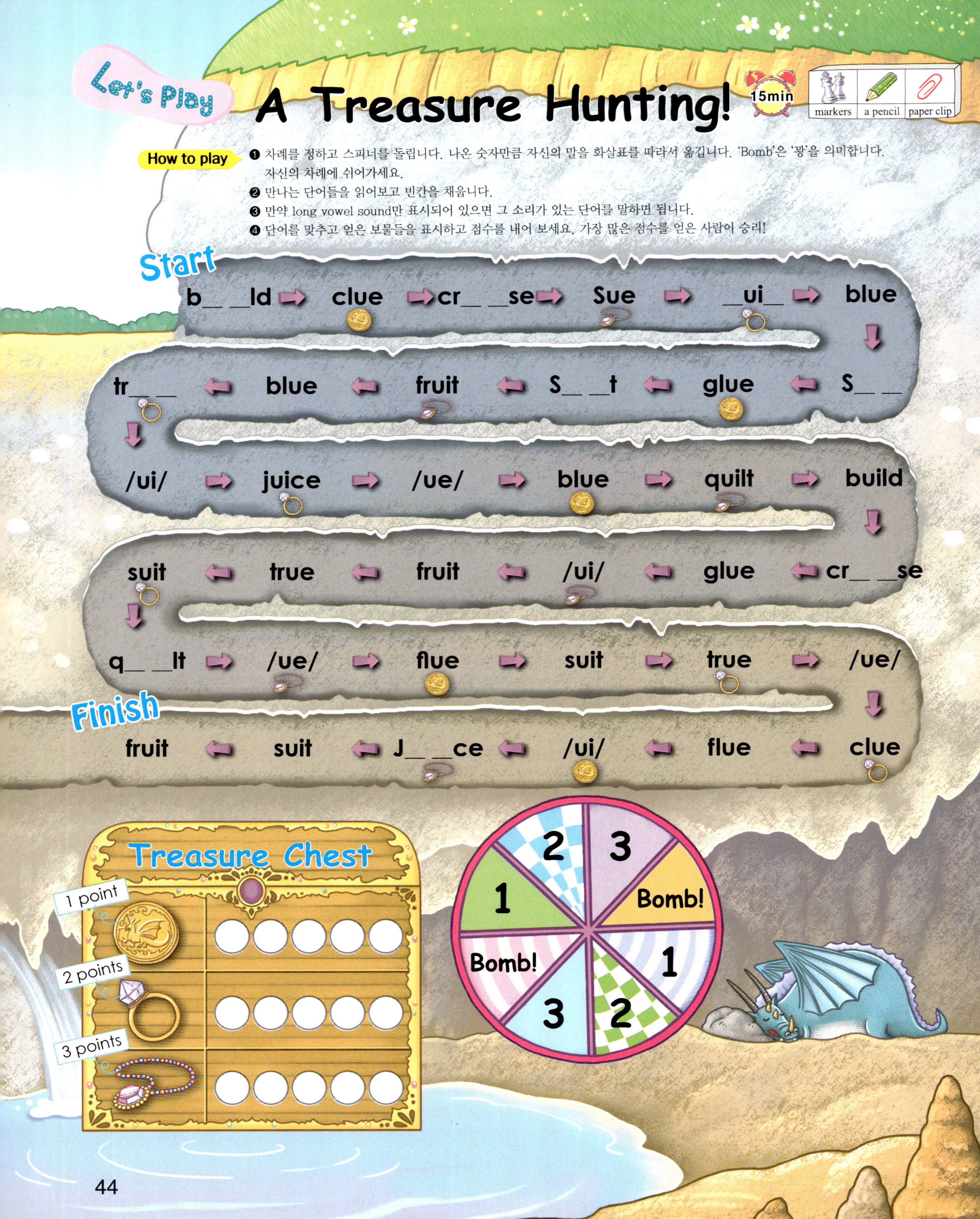
Let's Play
A Treasure Hunting!
15min
markers | a pencil | paper clip
How to play
❶ 차례를 정하고 스피너를 돌립니다. 나온 숫자만큼 자신의 말을 화살표를 따라서 옮깁니다. 'Bomb'은 '꽝'을 의미합니다.
자신의 차례에 쉬어가세요.
❷ 만나는 단어들을 읽어보고 빈칸을 채웁니다.
❸ 만약 long vowel sound만 표시되어 있으면 그 소리가 있는 단어를 말하면 됩니다.
❹ 단어를 맞추고 얻은 보물들을 표시하고 점수를 내어 보세요. 가장 많은 점수를 얻은 사람이 승리!
Start
b__ld → clue → cr___se → Sue → __ui__ → blue
tr___ ← blue ← fruit ← S__t ← glue ← S__
/ui/ → juice → /ue/ → blue → quilt → build
suit ← true ← fruit ← /ui/ ← glue ← cr___se
q___lt → /ue/ → flue → suit → true → /ue/
Finish
fruit ← suit ← J___ce ← /ui/ ← flue ← clue
Treasure Chest
1 point
2 points
3 points
2 3
1 Bomb!
Bomb! 1
3 2

Homework Spot `Track 48`

1 Listen. If the picture is correct, write ⭕. But if not, write ❌.

①    ②    ③ 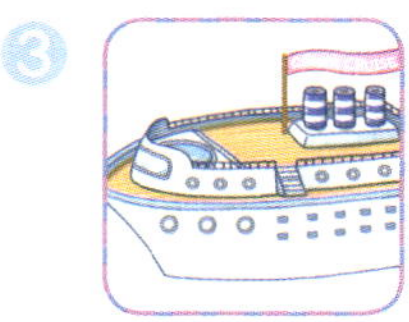

2 Listen and write the missing letters.

① fl ___ ___

② b ___ ___ ld

③ fr ___ ___ t

④ s ___ ___ t

⑤ gl ___ ___

⑥ S ___ ___

3 Listen and look at the picture. Then choose **Yes** or **No**.

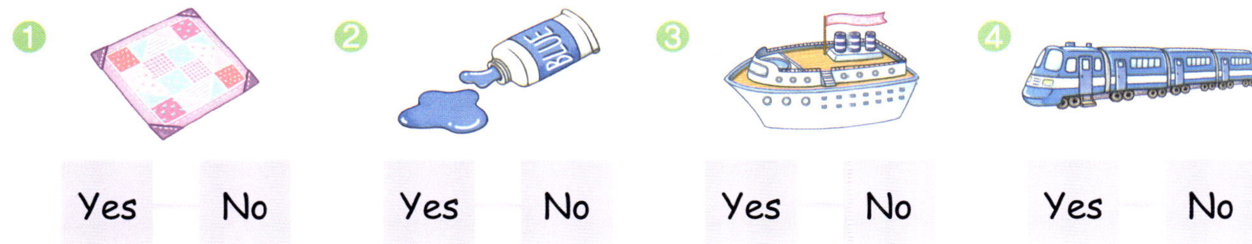

① Yes   No
② Yes   No
③ Yes   No
④ Yes   No

4 Read and fill in the blanks.

①  

Sue puts her photos in the album using __________ .

② 

It's fun to go on a __________ .

Consonant blends : nd, nt, ck

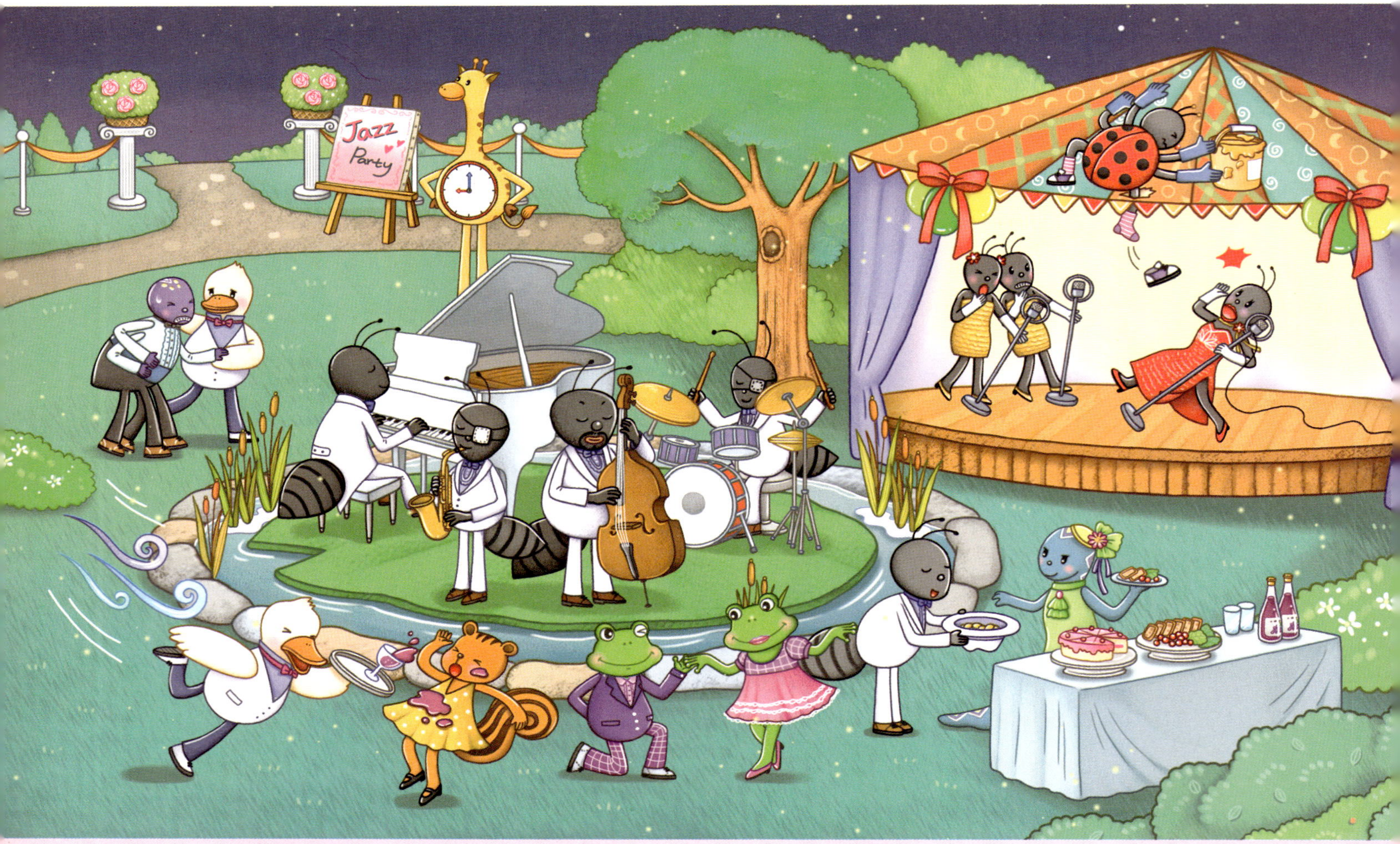

Look and find the new word, then circle.

Listen, repeat and check. **Track 49**

-nd		-nt		-ck	
hand ☐	stand ☐	cent ☐	paint ☐	black ☐	sick ☐
band ☐	pond ☐	tent ☐	ant ☐	clock ☐	sock ☐
wind ☐	blind ☐	want ☐	plant ☐	neck ☐	duck ☐

My Dictionary

Go for a Jolly Chant! Track 50

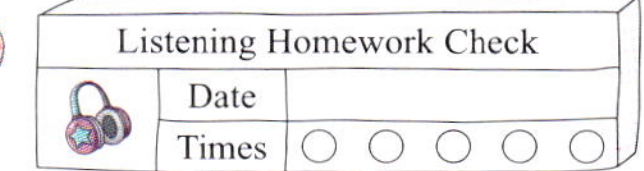

Verse 1

Give me an "N!" and a "D!"(Give me an "N!" and a "D!")
"N" and "D".("N" and "D".) Let's make the sound, /nd/, /nd/, sound!
/nd/, /nd/ stand! (/nd/, /nd/, stand!) /nd/, /nd/, blind! (/nd/, /nd/, blind!)
/nd/, /nd/ pond! (/nd/, /nd/, pond!) /nd/, wind! (/nd/, wind!)
/nd/, hand! (/nd/, hand!) /nd/, band! (/nd/, band!)
"nd", "nd" family! ("nd", "nd" family!)

Verse 2

Give me an "N!" and a "T!"
"N" and "T".
Let's make the sound,
/nt/, /nt/, sound!
/nt/, /nt/, paint(plant, want)!
/nt/, cent(tent, ant)!
"nt", "nt" family!

Verse 3

Give me a "C!" and a "K!"
"C" and "K".
Let's make the sound,
/ck/, /ck/, sound!
/ck/, /ck/, black(clock, duck)!
/ck/, neck(sick, sock)!
"ck", "ck" family!

POP QUIZ Listen, and circle the correct consonant blends sound. Track 51

Score / 6

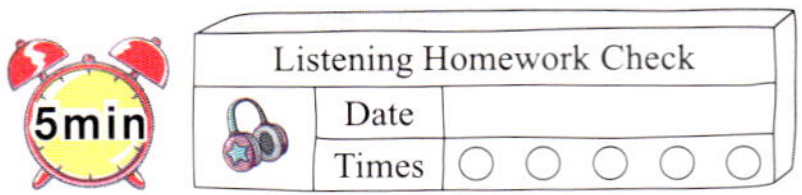

Listen and circle the correct picture. Track 52

Listen and circle the correct picture. Track 53

1.
2.
3.

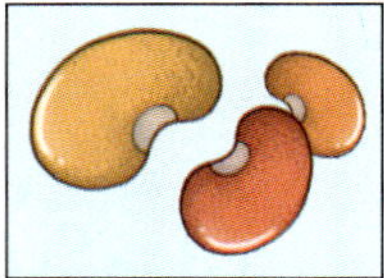

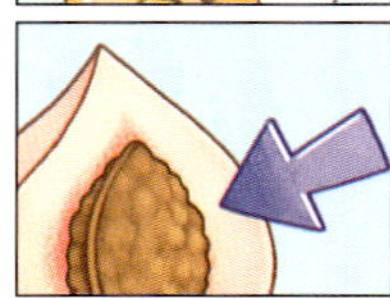

Listen and connect the picture. Track 54

1   2   3

Look at the given consonant blends. Then make nes words.

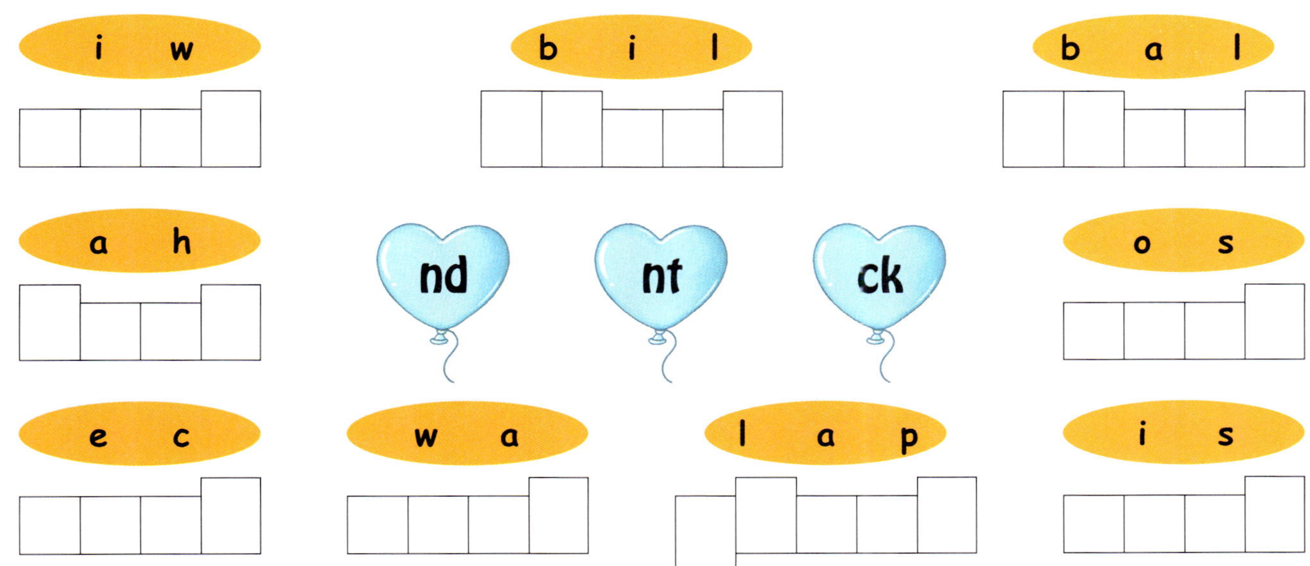

Look and write. Then choose the picture that has the different consonant blends sound.

MINI TEST   Read and write the word in the blank.

1. An ____________ s to play the saxophone.

2. A duck is ________ ing the wall ________ .

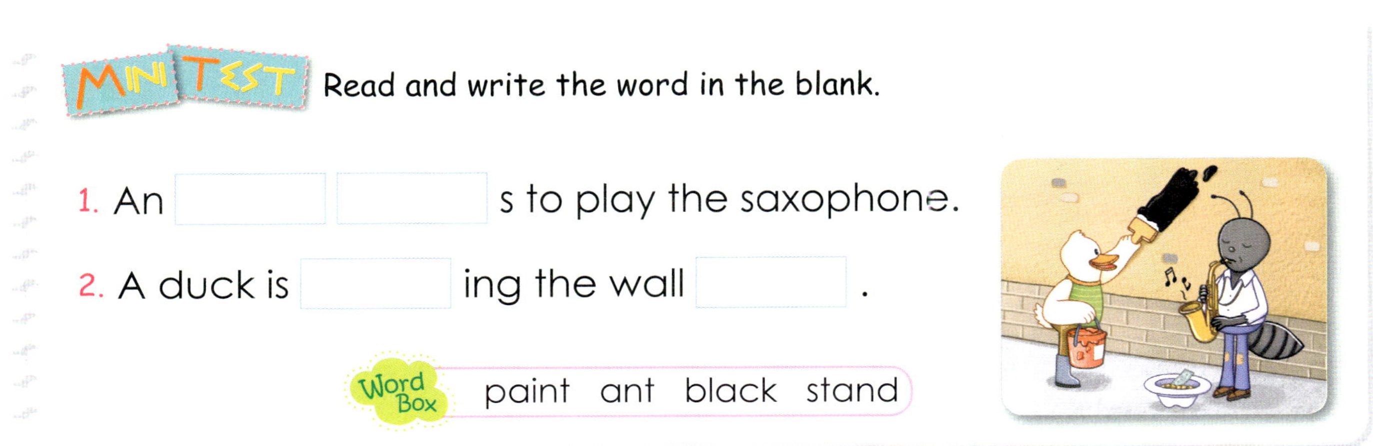

Word Box   paint   ant   black   stand

49

Let's Play

Flick to Take!

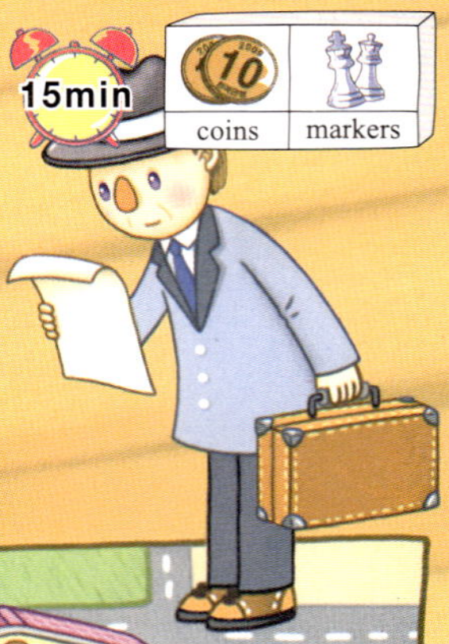

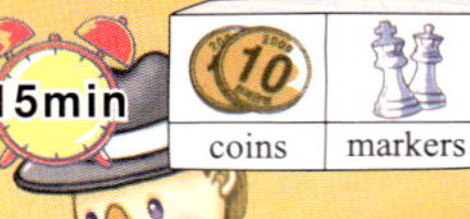

How to play

❶ 동전을 지도 위에서 튕겨서 동전이 도착하는 곳의 단어를 말하고 자신의 마커를 올려놓아서 그 지역을 삽니다.
❷ 만약 동전이 2~3구역에 걸치게 되면, 그 모든 구역의 단어를 말하고 지시를 따릅니다. 만약 모두 성공하면 그 칸들 위에 자신의 마커들을 개수만큼 올려 놓을 수 있습니다.
❸ 지시어를 만나게 되면 지시어를 따르되, 3초 안에 행동해야 합니다.

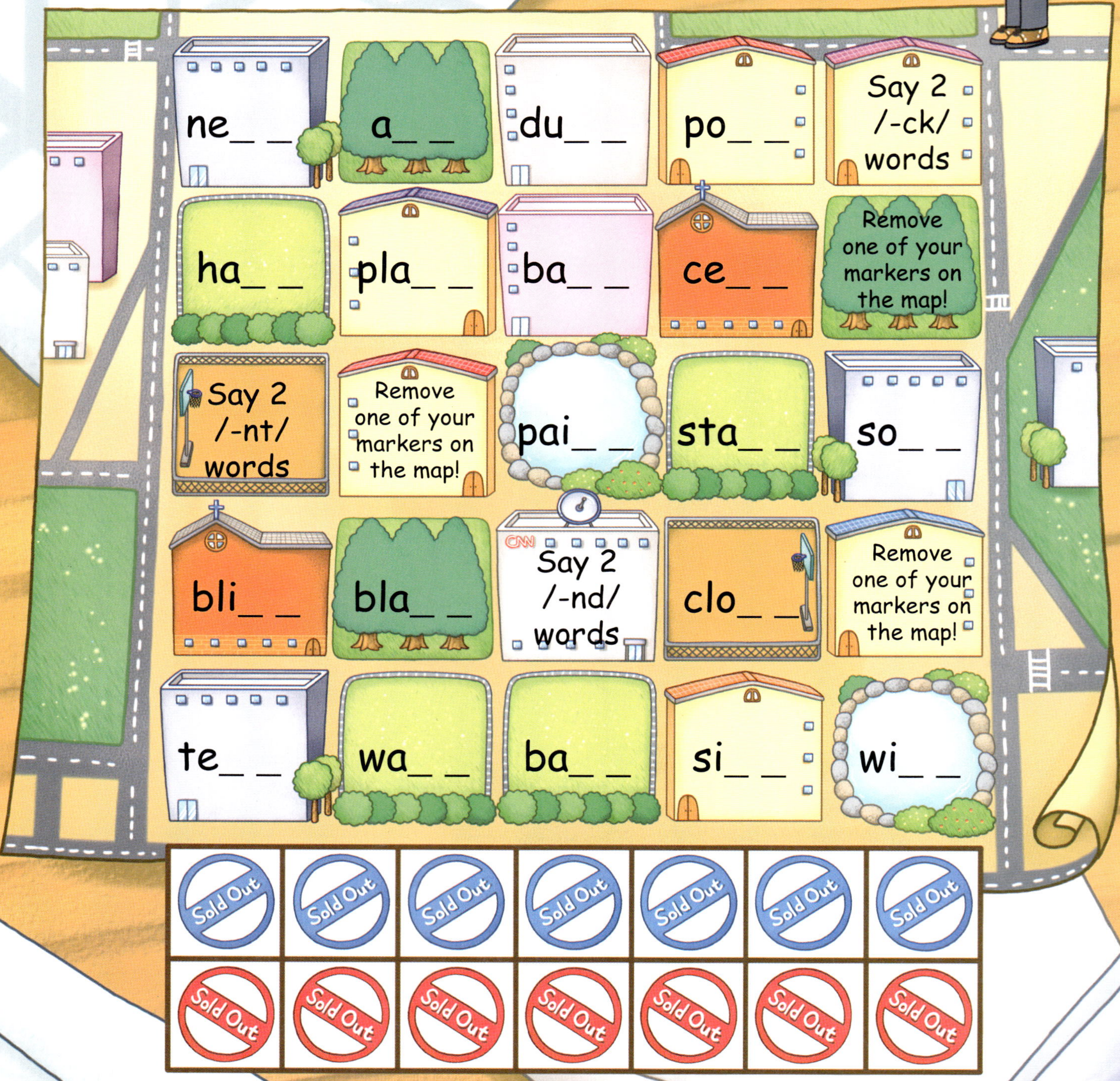

Track 55

1 Listen and connect the picture with the word that you hear.

1   2   3   4

2 Listen and match the common long vowel sound of the two words that you hear.

1 wa / ce   **2** te / pai

3 bla / so   **4** sta / wi

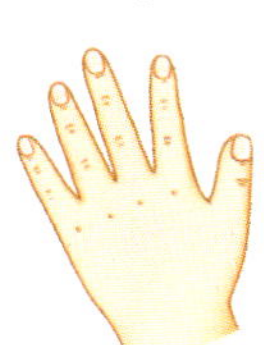

3 Do the crossword.

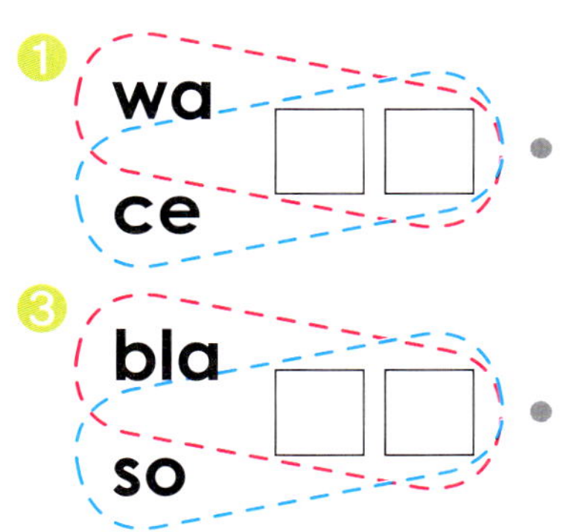

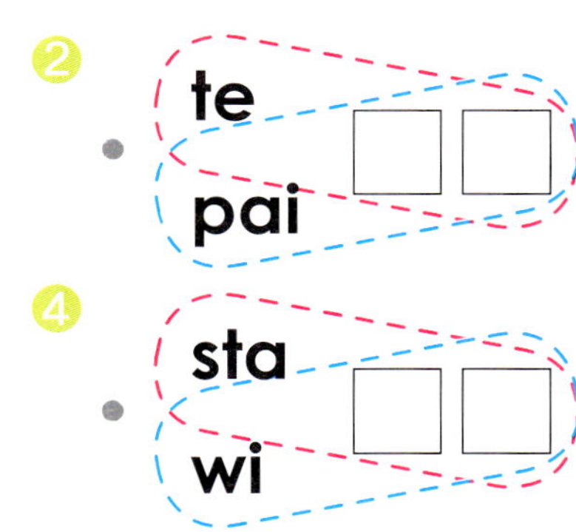

1   2   d   3 t   d

4   5   k   6   t   d

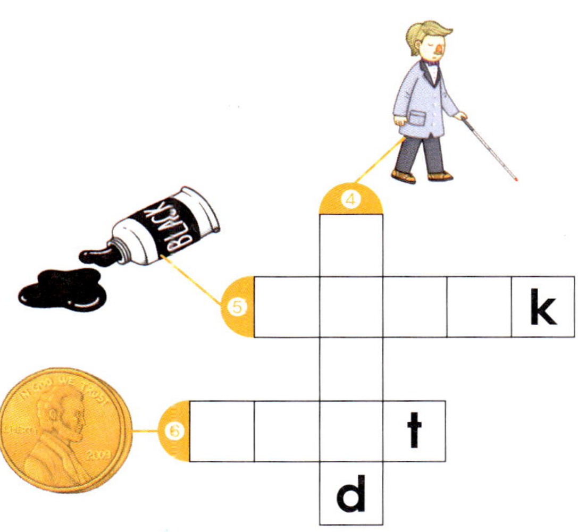

Unit 09

Consonant blends with l : bl, cl, fl, gl, pl, sl

10min

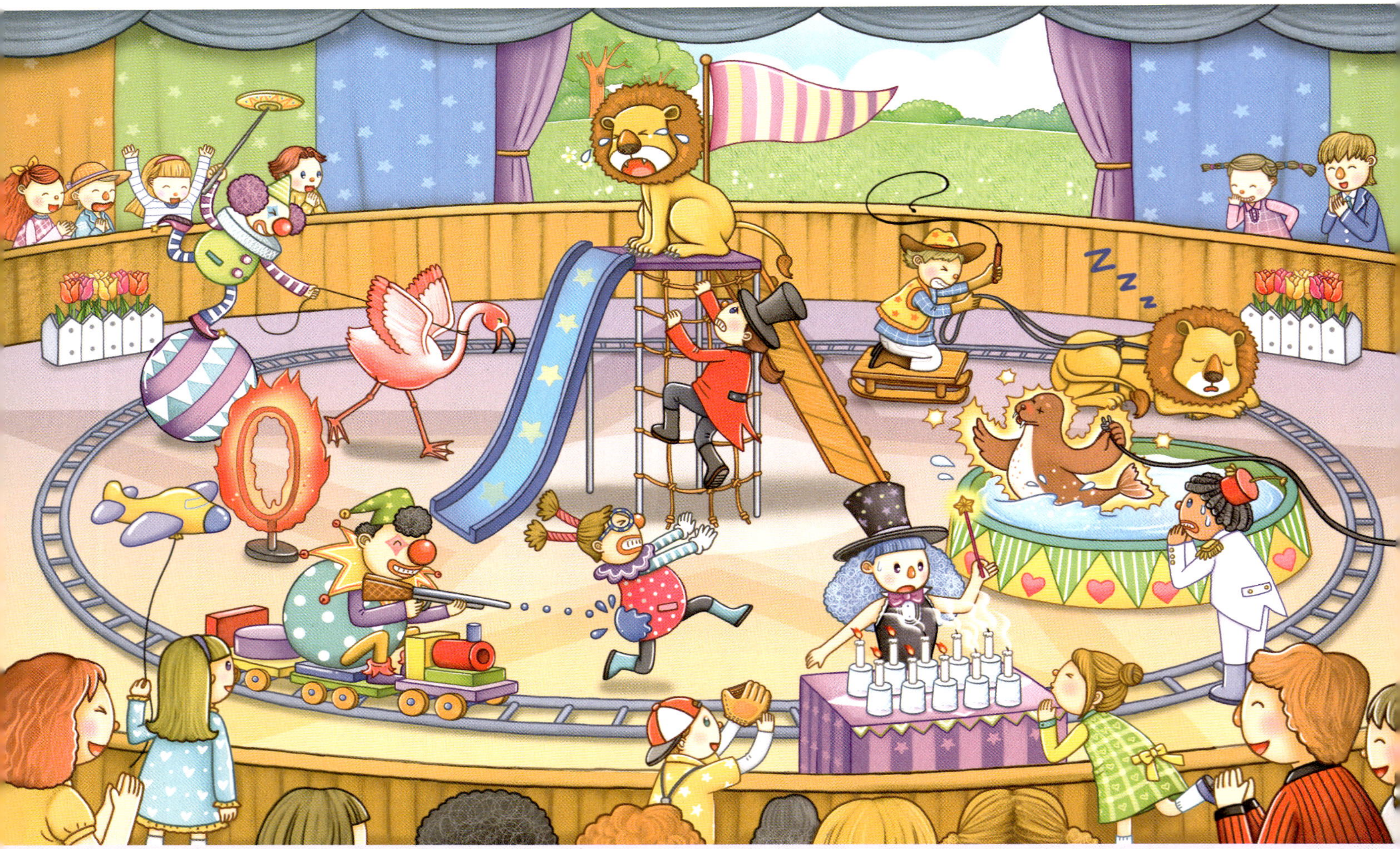

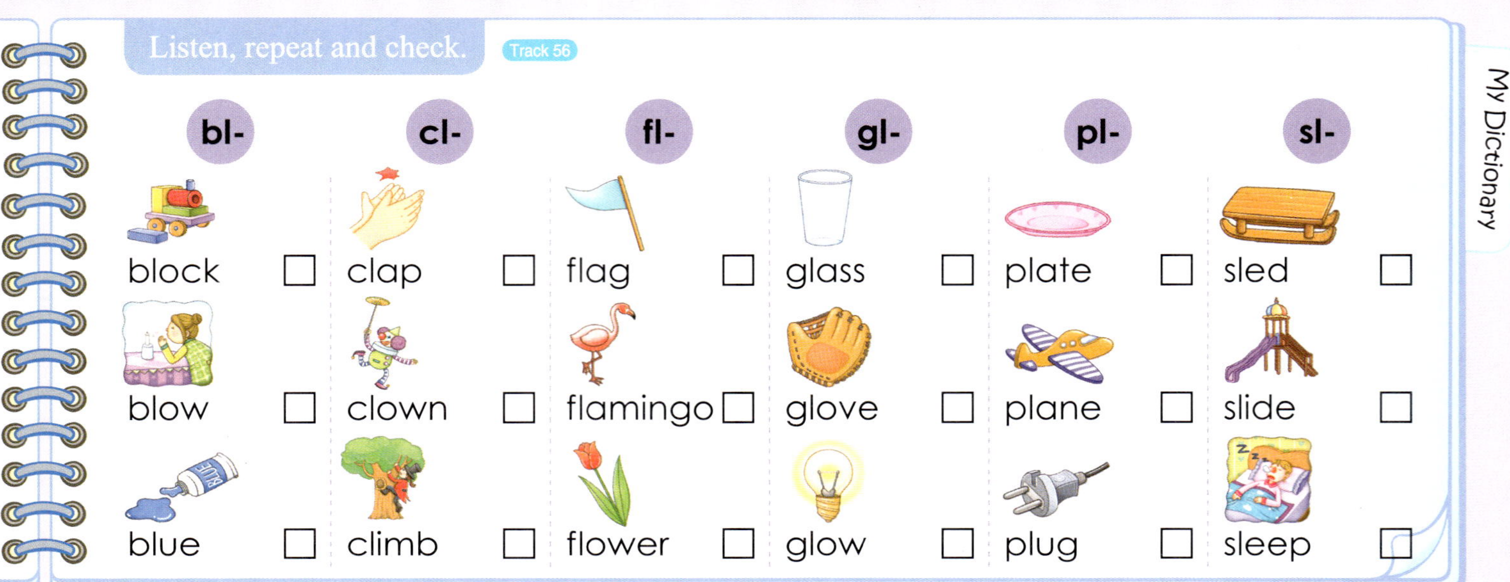

Look and find the new word, then circle.

Listen, repeat and check. Track 56

bl-	cl-	fl-	gl-	pl-	sl-
block ☐	clap ☐	flag ☐	glass ☐	plate ☐	sled ☐
blow ☐	clown ☐	flamingo ☐	glove ☐	plane ☐	slide ☐
blue ☐	climb ☐	flower ☐	glow ☐	plug ☐	sleep ☐

My Dictionary

At the Higgledy-Piggledy Circus!  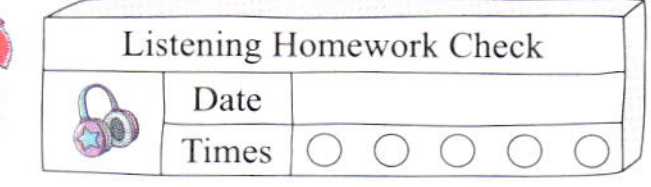

Here are many flags 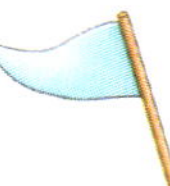 and flowers  .

A clown on the block train

and a flamingo on a plate .

People clap but a man sleeps .

A seal blows a candle on a glass .

Lions slide on a sled .

It's so funny, isn't it?

Plug me in a higgledy-piggledy circus.

POP QUIZ Listen, and write the missing letters. Track 58

Score / 6

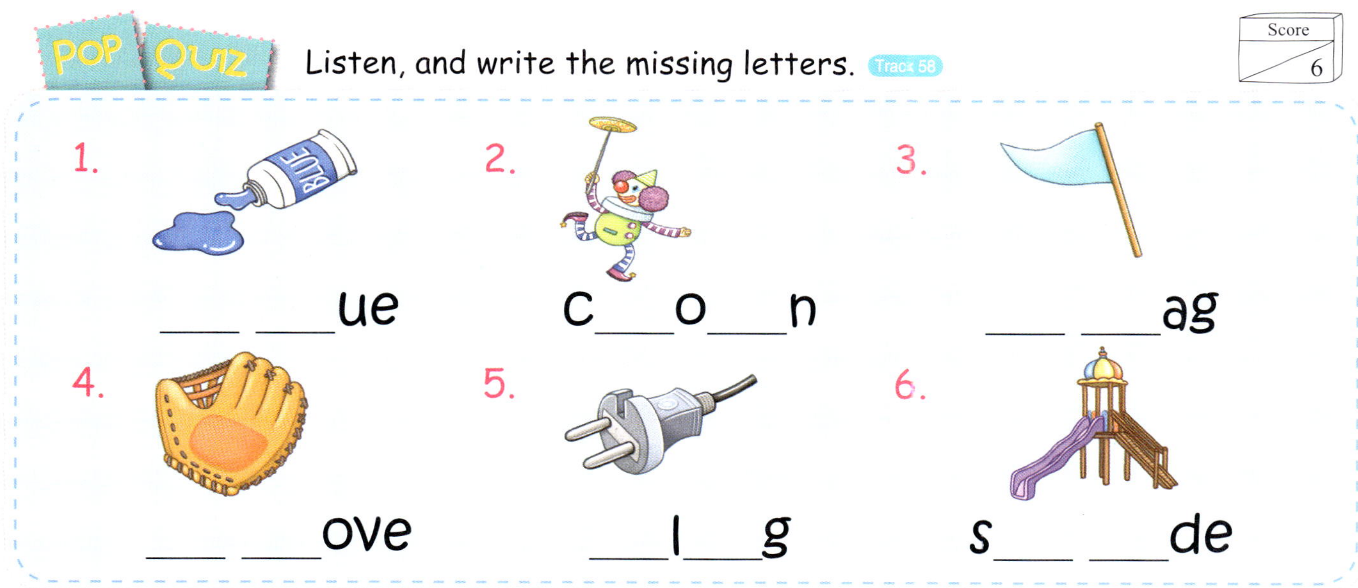

1. _____ _____ue

2. c_____o_____n

3. _____ _____ag

4. _____ _____ove

5. _____l_____g

6. s_____ _____de

L isten and number in order. `Track 59`

L isten and circle the correct word. `Track 60`

1. boue
   brue
   blue

2. flower
   flawer
   falwer

3. grow
   glow
   grab

4. prane
   plane
   palne

5. sled
   sleed
   seld

6. cream
   clam
   climb

L isten. If the picture is correct, write ◯ . But if not, write ✗ . `Track 61`

1.

2.

3.

4.

Find two pictures that begin with the same sound. Then choose their common beginning sound.

1. bl fl pl sl cl gl

2. bl fl cl sl pl gl

3. bl fl cl sl pl gl

Look at the picture and find the correct word.

p	k	r	a
t	l	a	k
p	a	u	v
b	h	i	g

w	n	r	a
t	r	i	k
f	l	a	g
g	e	z	e

o	p	b	q
x	i	l	k
z	g	o	u
r	f	w	t

Read the sentences and choose the correct word.

1. A block is in a grove / glove .
2. A crane / clown is on a slide / slid .
3. A girl has a brue / blue flag.

Let's Play
The Lion Circus!
15min
a die | markers | a pencil | paper clip
How to play
❶ 주사위를 던지고 이동하면서 단어들을 크게 읽습니다.
❷ Finish에 먼저 도착하는 사람이 승리!
Start
NO!
NO!
plane
YES!
Finish
sled
glow
blue
Try Again With Spin! Spin!
❶ 스피너를 돌려서 나온 자음으로 단어를 만들어서 맞게 말하면 자신의
차트에 그 자음 부분을 체크합니다.
❷ 먼저 차트를 모두 체크한 사람이 승리!
bl
ql
sl
Bomb!
Bomb!
pl
fl
cl
Consonant Blends Chart
BL
CL
FL
GL
PL
SL
56

1 Listen. If the word pair has the same consonant sound, write ◯.
If not, write ✗.

1 ☐ **2** ☐ **3** ☐ **4** ☐

2 Listen and connect the pictures to the correct consonant blends sounds.

bl   **fl**   **cl**   **pl**   **gl**   **sl**

3 Listen and choose the correct words.

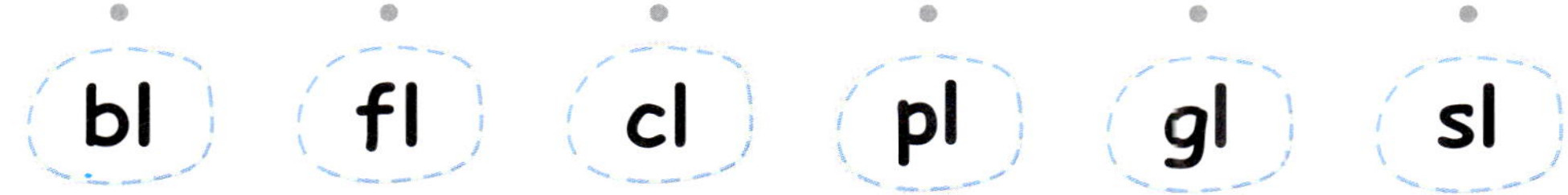

1 A _______ is _______ ing.   `clown  slang  sleep`

2 He has a _______ and a _______ train.   `brock  glove  block`

3 There are some _______ s under the _______ .   `sride  plate  slide`

4 Read and fill in the blank.

1 A boy _______ s out at the candles.

2 A girl _______ s her hands.

Consonant blends with r : br, cr, fr, dr, pr ,tr

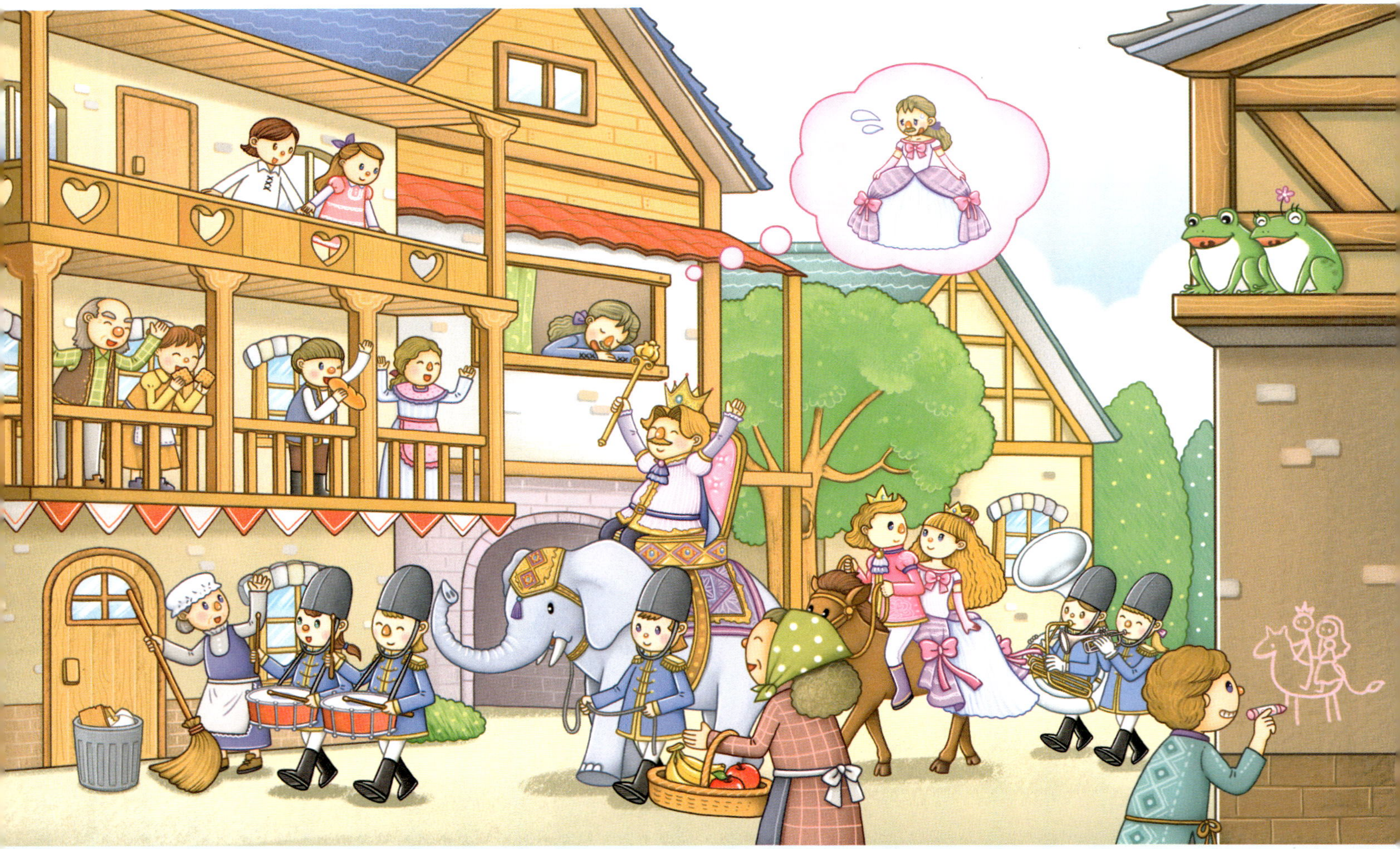

Look and find the new word, then circle.

br-		cr-		dr-		fr-		pr-		tr-	
brass	☐	crown	☐	dress	☐	frog	☐	prince	☐	tree	☐
bread	☐	cracker	☐	dream	☐	friend	☐	princess	☐	trash	☐
broom	☐	crayon	☐	drum	☐	fruit	☐	pretty	☐	trunk	☐

 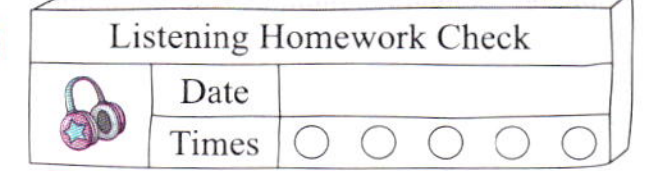
10min — Listening Homework Check — Date — Times ○ ○ ○ ○ ○

Unit 10

With a **drum** and a **brass** band,

The royal parade begins.

A **prince**  and a **princess**  are **dressed**  up.

How fantastic it is!

Between the **tree**s ,

A **pretty**  girl and her **friend**  are happy.

Between the buildings,

A woman with a **broom**  is happy.

A man is dreaming a **dream** .

Maybe he is happy, too.

How fantastic it is!

POP QUIZ Listen, and circle the missing letters. Track 65

Score / 6

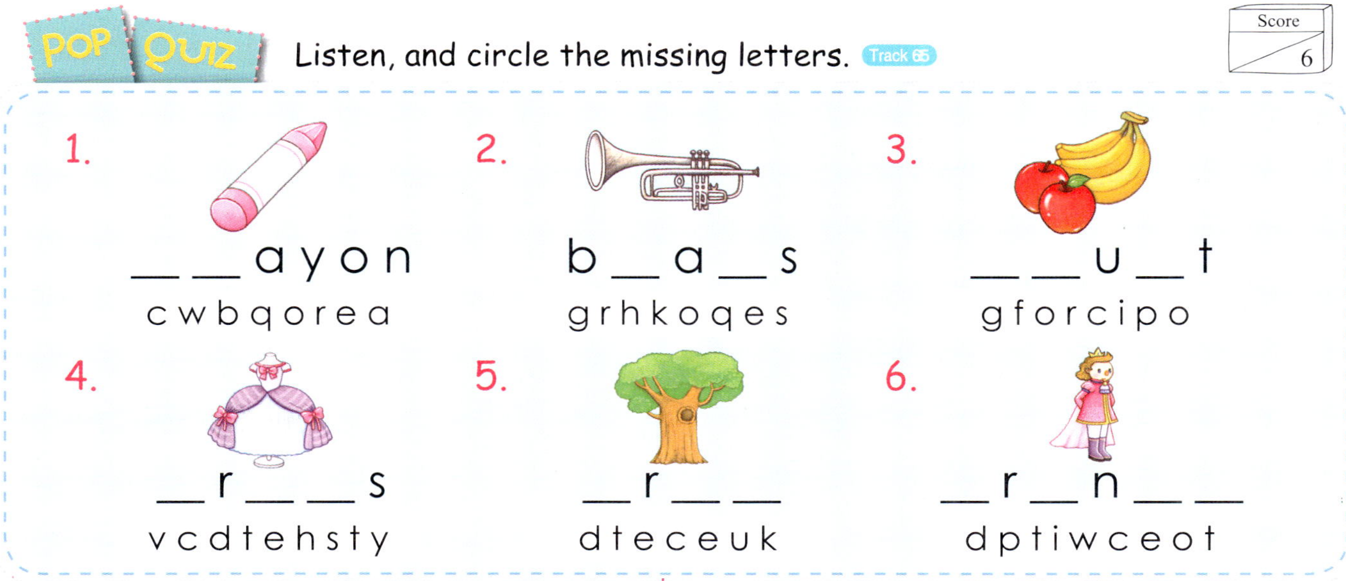

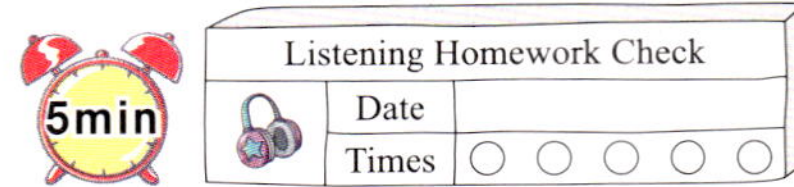

L isten and circle the correct word. Track 66

1. bried
   brain
   bread

2. crag
   cracker
   crunch

3. fried
   french
   friend

4. dream
   drain
   dry

5. print
   pretty
   practic

6. trunk
   trunt
   truck

L isten and check the correct consonant blends words. Track 67

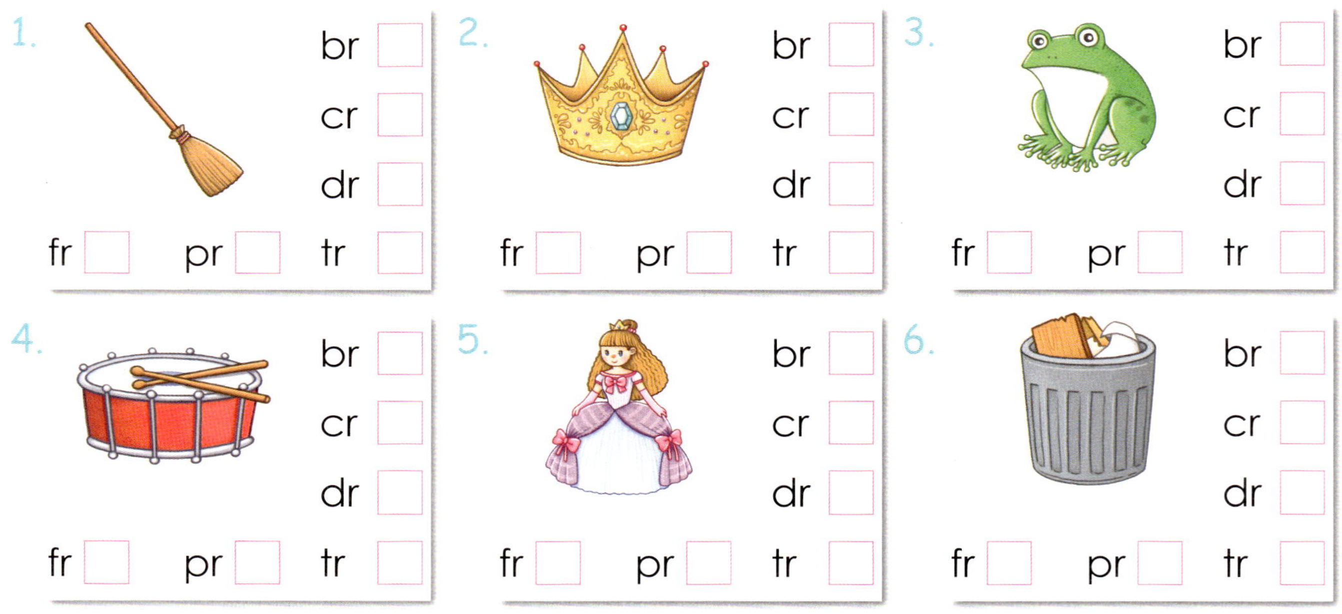

L isten and number in order. Track 68

Read the pictures and unscramble the words.

1.

______

d e r a m

2.

______

r a s b s

3.

______

r f g o

4.

______

s t h r a

5.

______

c k r e r a c

6.

______

i r p n e c

Check the correct word.

1. 	2. 	3. 
○ creyon ○ crayon ○ caryon	○ dram ○ dum ○ drum	○ trank ○ trunk ○ trenk

 **MINI TEST** Read and choose the words by the pictures.

1. A baby eats clackers / crackers .

2. The prince / princess is pretty / prenty .

3. Two goats / gates eat test / toast .

4. A drum / drem band is under the trass / tree .

62

1 Listen and check the correct picture.

2 Listen and draw a line to match the picture to the correct word.

3 Listen and circle the letter for its consonant blends sound.

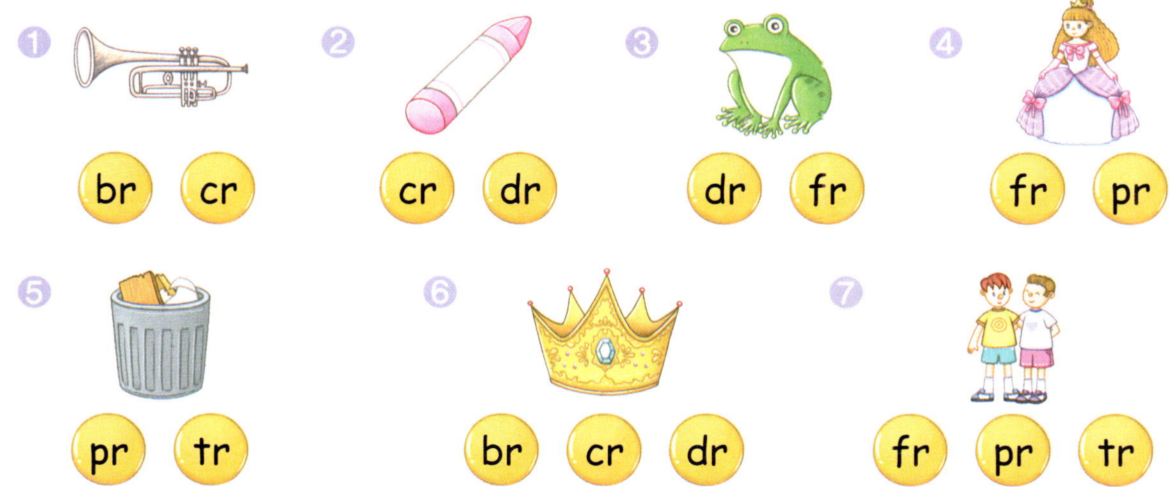

Consonant blends with s : sm, sn, st, sw, sp

10min

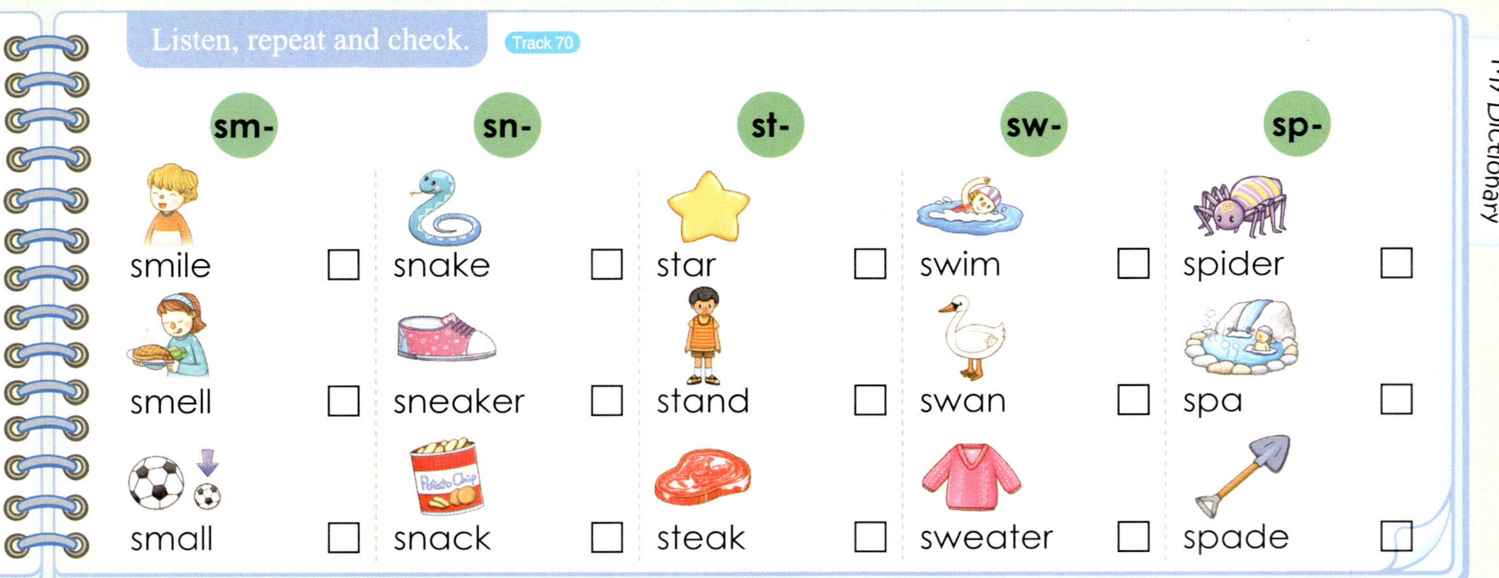

Look and find the new word, then circle.

Listen, repeat and check. Track 70

sm-	sn-	st-	sw-	sp-
smile ☐	snake ☐	star ☐	swim ☐	spider ☐
smell ☐	sneaker ☐	stand ☐	swan ☐	spa ☐
small ☐	snack ☐	steak ☐	sweater ☐	spade ☐

My Dictionary

Sing a Joyful Song! Track 71

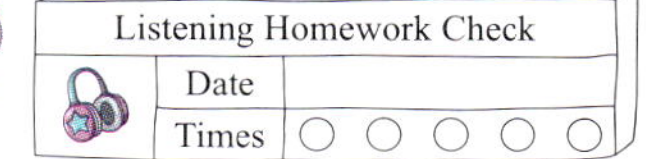

Where's Smith's Sneaker?

Twinkling stars  in the night sky.

The hugger-mugger spa in the bush.

A spider and a snake in a sneaker .

Small ants swim in a lunch box.

The swans wear sweaters .

Twinkling stars in the night sky.

The hugger-mugger spa in the bush.

Where's Smith's sneaker ?

Where's Smith's sneaker ?

I got it in the hugger-mugger spa .

POP QUIZ Listen, and follow the words through the maze. Track 72

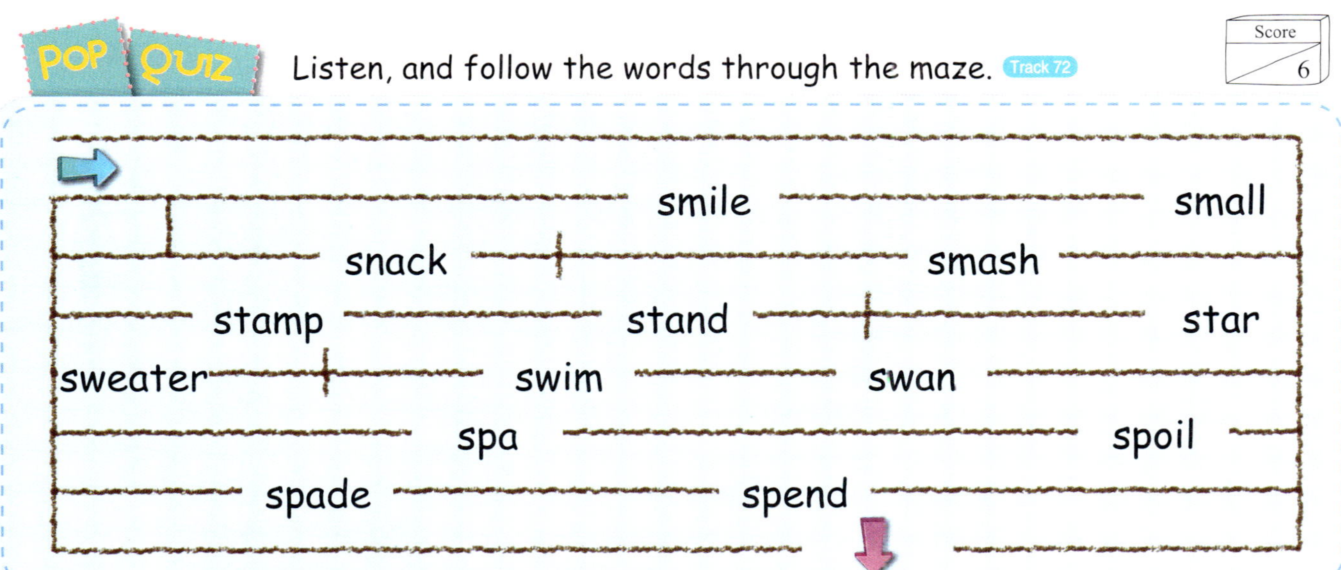

Listen and check(✔) the correct picture. `Track 73` 5min

Listen and connect the each picture to the correct consonant blends sound. `Track 74`

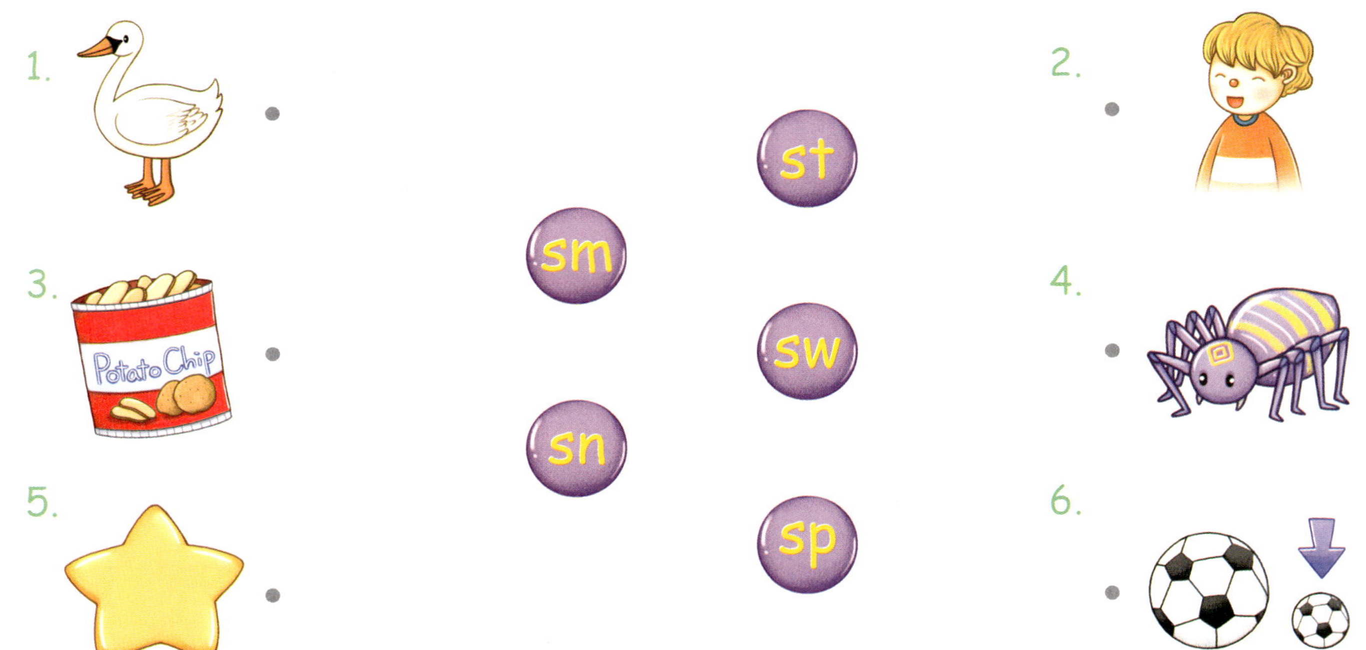

Listen and choose the correct word that has the cosonant blends sound. `Track 75`

1. smell
   smart
   small

2. snapped
   sneaker
   sniffer

3. stamp
   stump
   stand

4. spank
   spade
   spen

Read the name of each picture below. Write each beginning consonant blends.

Read the pictures and circle the one that has a different consonant blends sound.

 Write the correct word in the blank.

1. A spider __________ s in the spa.

2. __________ lost one of his __________ s.

3. A __________ wears a __________ .

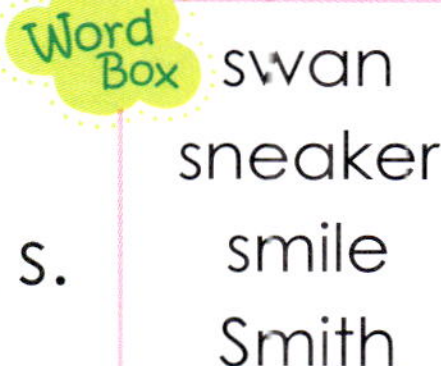

Let's Play
Memory Game!
15min
Potato Chip
Potato Chip
My Word List

How to play
① 게임순서를 정하고 카드를 모두 잘라낸다.
② 카드를 뒤집어 놓고 차례대로 2장씩 카드를 뒤집어 본다.
③ 뒤집은 2장의 카드가 같은 카드일 경우, 그 카드의 이름을
  말하고 My Word List에 그 이름을 적은 후 가져온다.
  만약 이름을 말하지 못하거나, My Word List에 적지
  못하면 그 카드는 다시 제자리에 놓는다.
④ 제일 먼저 My Word List를 채운 사람이 승리!

1 Listen and write ◯ or ✗.

2 Listen and write the missing letters.

3 Listen and choose **Yes** or **No**.

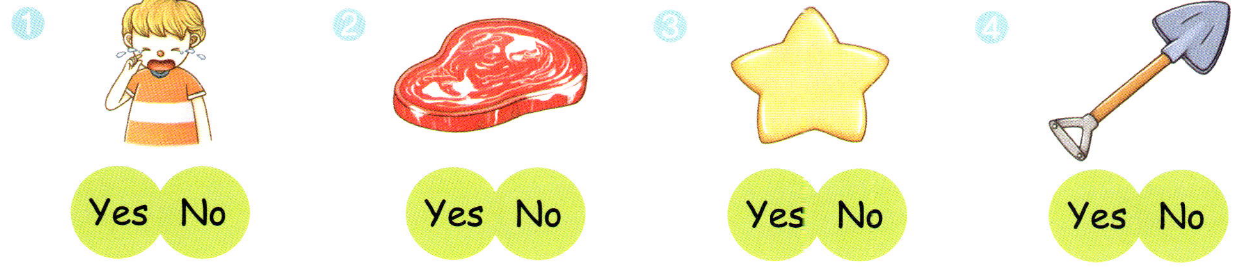

4 Read and choose the picture. Then fill in the blank.

The steak __________ s tasty.

The swan __________ s well.

Unit 12

Consonant blends with s : sc, sk, scr, spr, str

10min

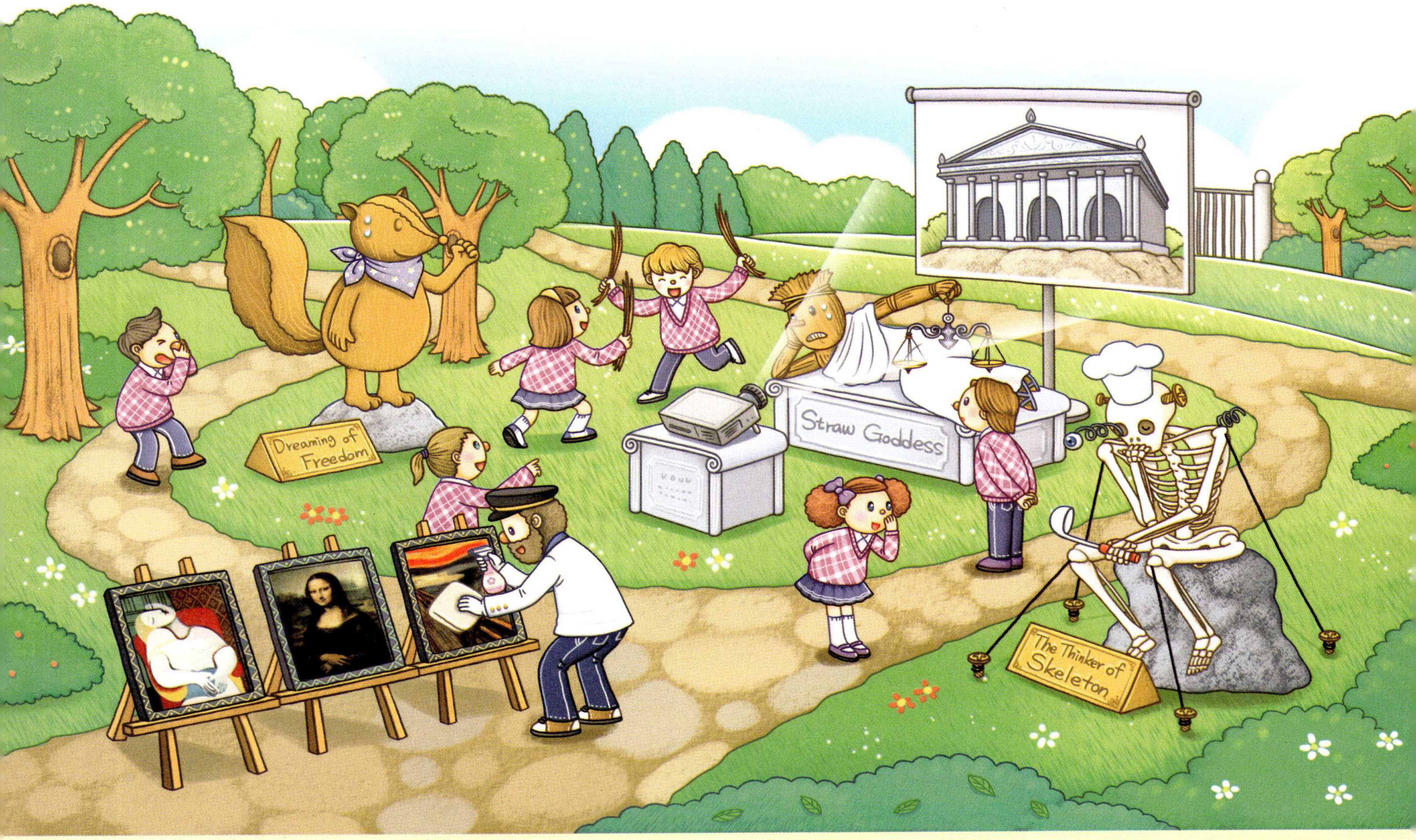

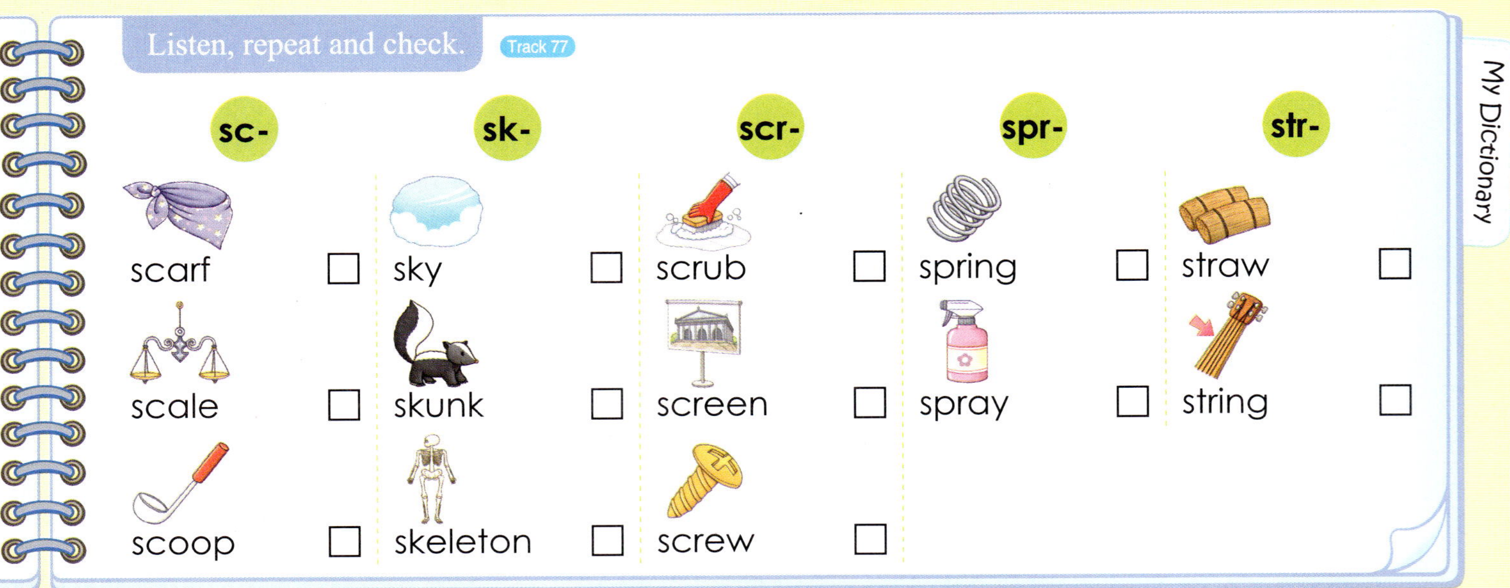

Look and find the new word, then circle.

My Dictionary

Listen, repeat and check. Track 77

sc-	sk-	scr-	spr-	str-
scarf ☐	sky ☐	scrub ☐	spring ☐	straw ☐
scale ☐	skunk ☐	screen ☐	spray ☐	string ☐
scoop ☐	skeleton ☐	screw ☐		

An Odd Poem Track 78

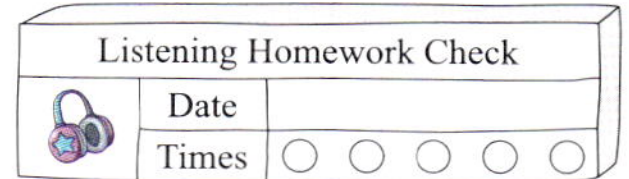

At the Art Gallery...

A skunk  with a scarf

Under the blue sky .

It looks nervous.

The straw goddess with a scale .

She looks nervous.

A skeleton with a scoop .

Screws , springs , and strings are from it.

He looks nervous.

We are not sure why…

But they look nervous.

POP QUIZ Listen, and circle the correct consonant blends sound. Track 79

Score
6

71

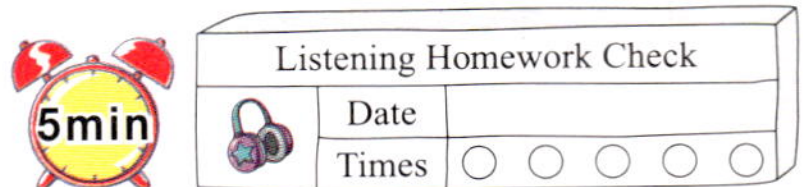

Listen and circle the correct picture. Track 80

1.
2.
3.
4.

Listen and circle the correct picture. Track 81

1.
2.
3.

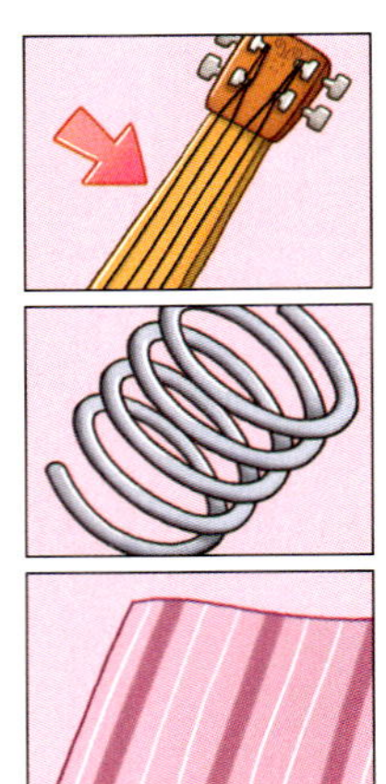

Listen and connect the picture that has the same consonant blends sound. Track 82

1.
2.
3.

72

Look at the given consonant blends and make new words using them. **5min**

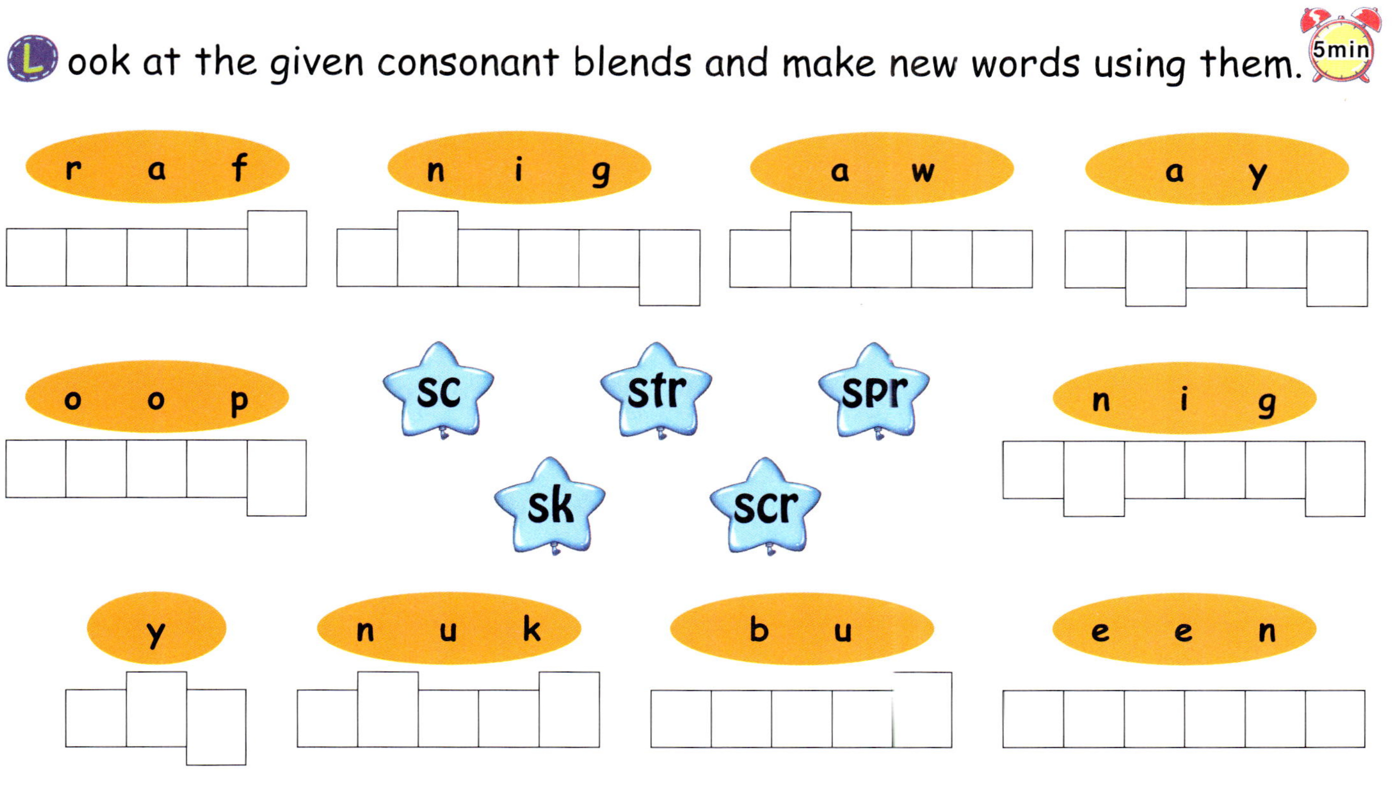

r a f

n i g

a w

a y

o o p

sc   str   spr

sk   scr

n i g

y

n u k

b u

e e n

Read the picture and choose the picture that has the different consonant blends sound.

1.

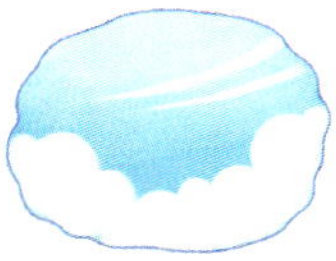

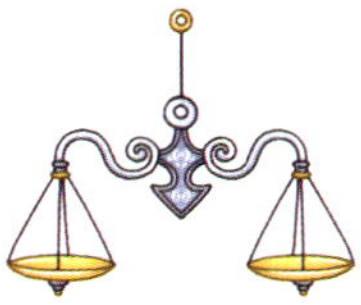

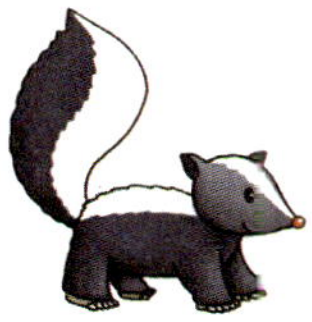

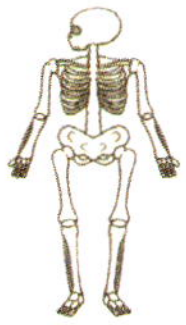

2.

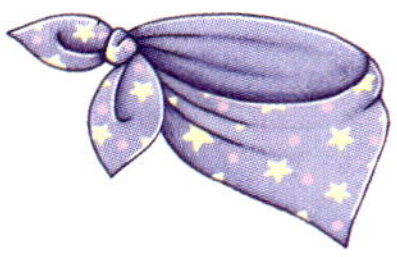

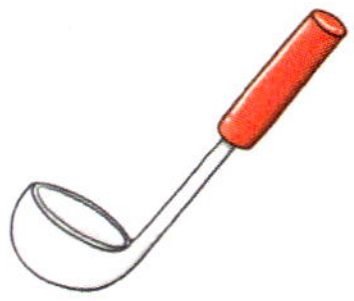

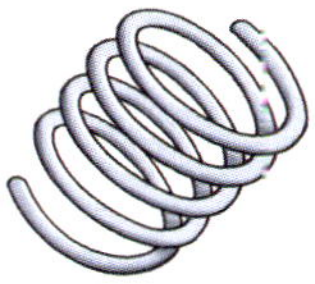

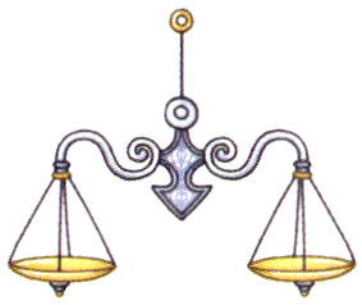

Read and fill in the blank.

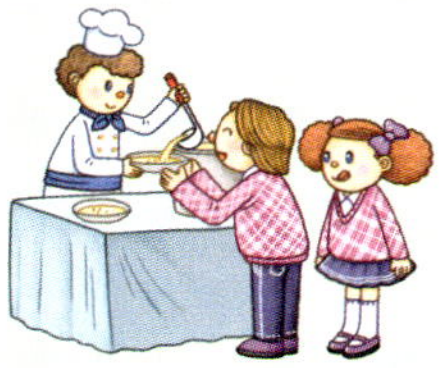

1. A cook serves soup using a [   ].

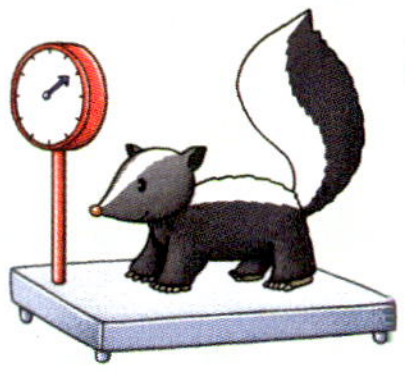

2. A [   ] is on the [   ].

scale   skunk   scoop

73

Flick to Buy!

		_ _rew	_ _reen	_ _y	
	_ _ray				_ _rub
_ _arf		_ _oop	Say 1 /sk-/ word	_ _ale		_ _oop
_ _raw	_ _ring				_ _ray	_ _unk
Say 1 /spr-/ word		Remove one of your makers on the map!	_ _ring	_ _oop		_ _rew
	_ _unk	_ _arf	_ _ _y	_ _ring	_ _reen	
_ _ale					_ _arf	Remove one of your makers on the map!
	_ _ring	_ _ring	_ _rew	Remove one of your makers on the map!		
Say 1 /sc-/ word	_ _ring				_ _ring	_ _ale
		_ _oop	_ _arf	_ _raw	_ _eleton	
_ _ _y	_ _rub					_ _ring
		_ _rew	Remove one of your makers on the map!	Say 1 /scr-/ word	Say 1 /str-/ word	
	_ _raw					
		_ _reen	_ _unk	_ _rub		

How to play

❶ 동전을 튕겨서 동전이 도착하는 곳의 단어를 말하고 자신의 마커를 올려놓아서 그 작품을 삽니다.

❷ 만약 동전이 2~3구역에 걸치게 되면, 그 모든 구역의 단어를 말하고 지시를 따릅니다. 만약 모두 성공하면 그 칸들 위에 자신의 마커들을 개수만큼 올려 놓을 수 있습니다. (마커 대신 색펜으로 X 표시해도 됩니다.)

❸ 지시어를 만나게 되면 지시어를 따르되, 3초 안에 행동해야 합니다.

Homework Spot

Track 83

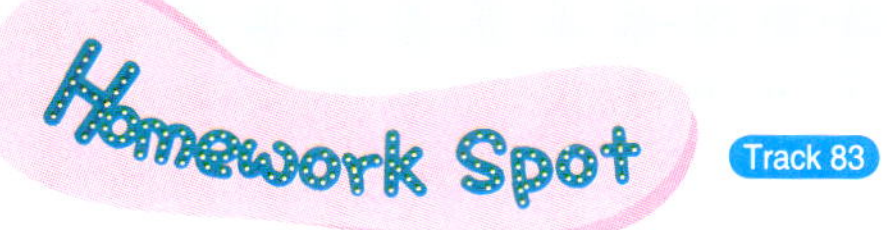

1 Listen and connect the picture with the word that you hear.

1 2 3 4

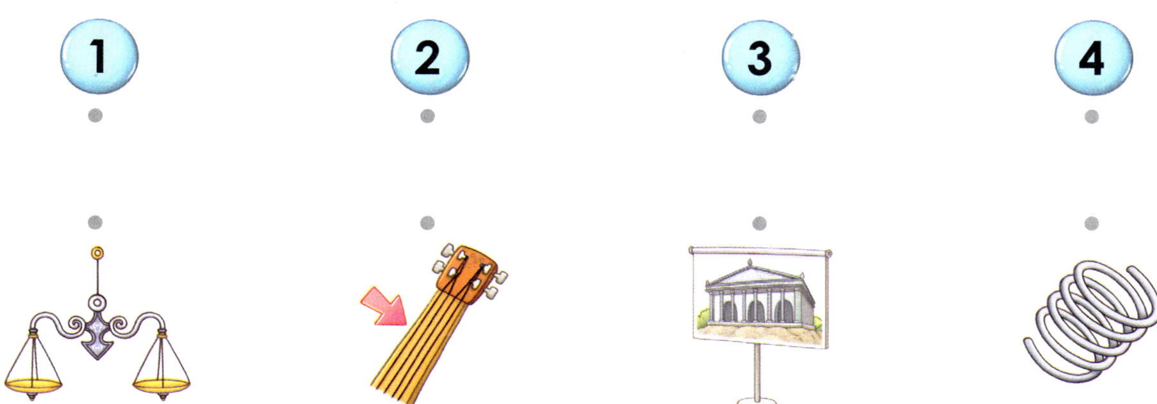

2 Listen and match the common consonant blends sound.

① ☐☐☐ aw / ing	scr	② ☐☐☐ ub / ew
	sk	
③ ☐☐ y / eleton	spr	④ ☐☐☐ ay / ing
	str	

3 Do the crossword.

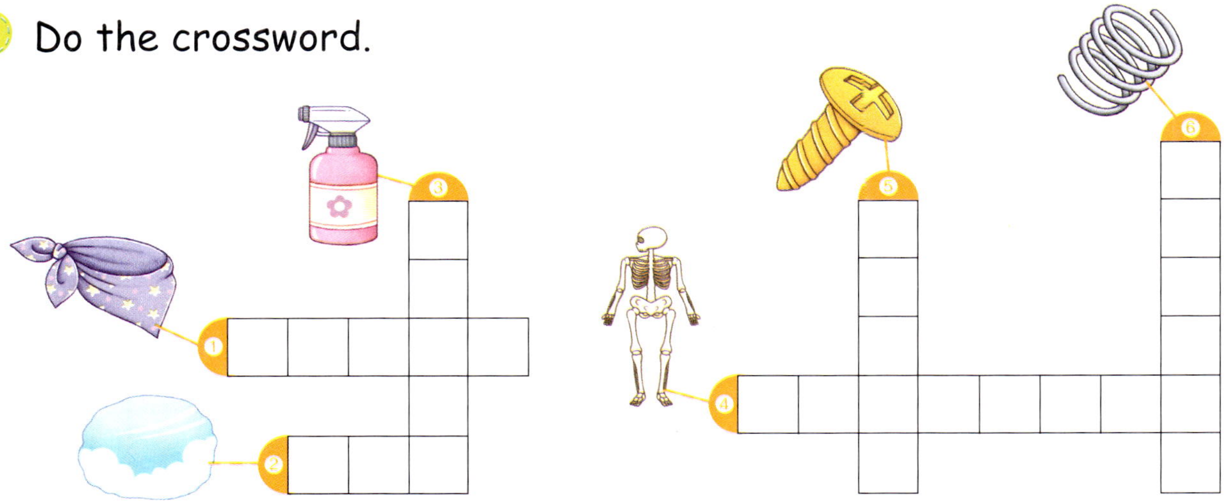

Unit 1

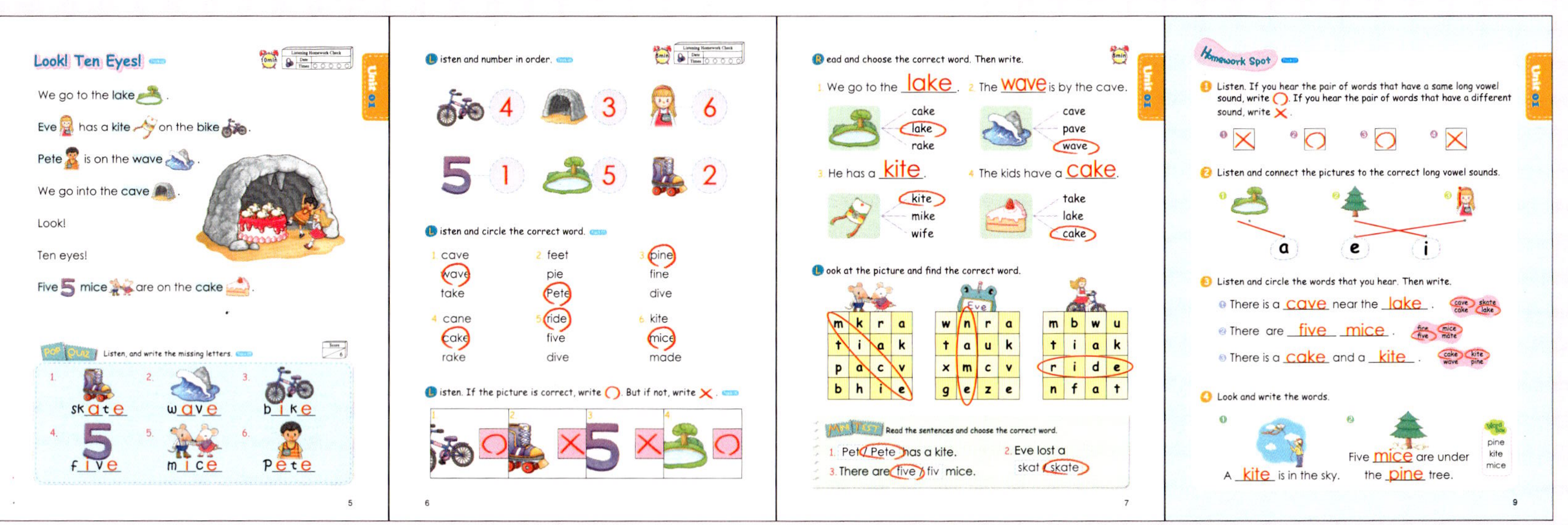

Unit 2

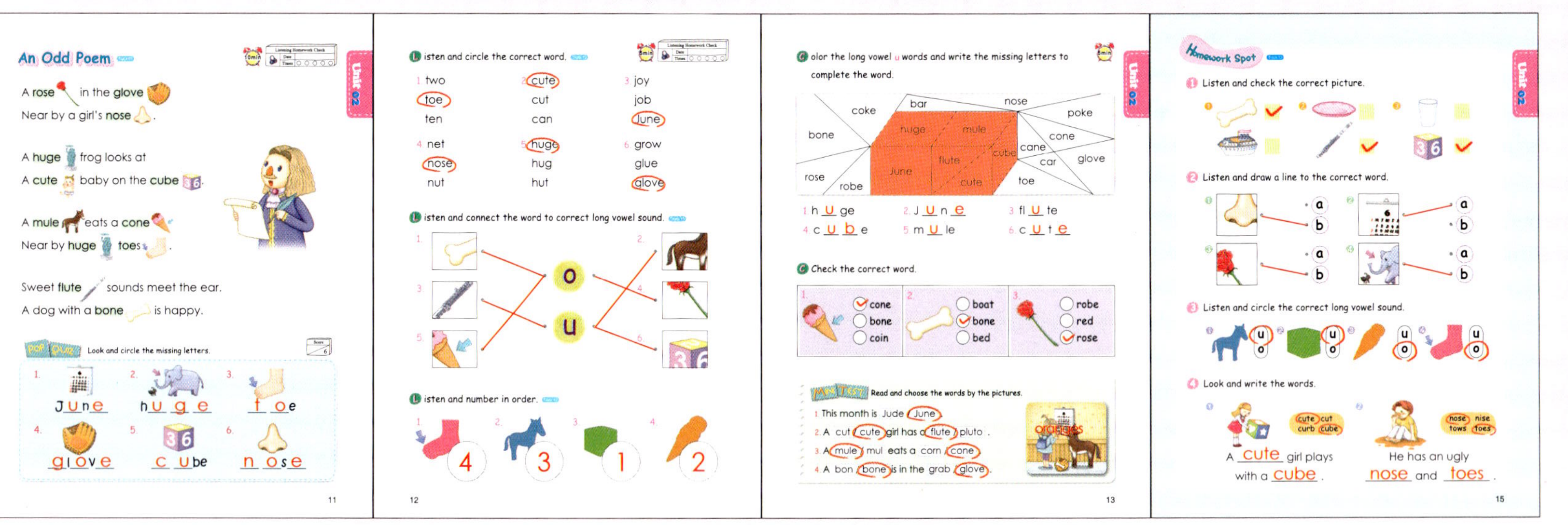

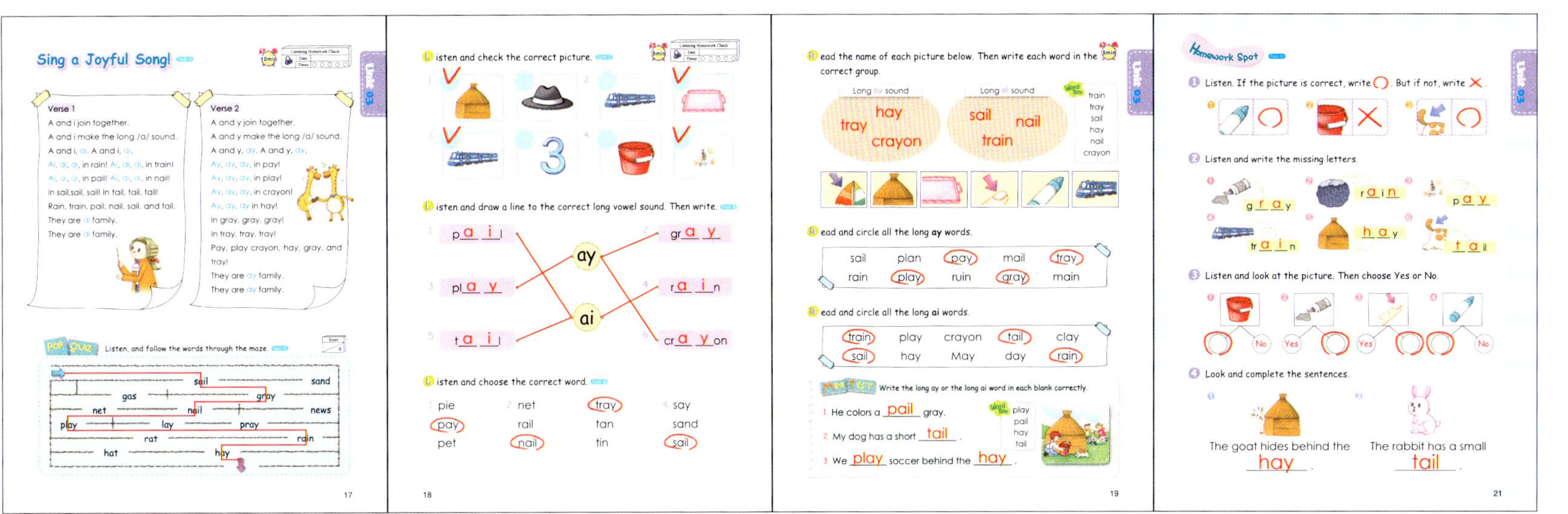

Unit 3

Sing a Joyful Song!

Verse 1
A and i join together.
A and i make the long /a/ sound.
A and i, ai. A and i, ai.
Ai, ai, ai, in rain! Ai, ai, ai, in train!
Ai, ai, ai, in pail! Ai, ai, ai, in nail!
In sail, sail, sail In tail, tail, tail!
Rain, train, pail, nail, sail, and tail.
They are a family.
They are a family.

Verse 2
A and y join together.
A and y make the long /a/ sound.
A and y, ay. A and y, ay.
Ay, ay, ay, in pay!
Ay, ay, ay, in play!
Ay, ay, ay, in crayon!
Ay, ay, ay, in hay!
In gray, gray, gray!
In tray, tray, tray!
Pay, play crayon, hay, gray, and tray!
They are ay family.
They are ay family.

POP QUIZ Listen, and follow the words through the maze.

sail — sand
gas — gray
net — nail — news
play — lay — pray
rat — rain
hat — hay

17

Listen and check the correct picture.

Listen and draw a line to the correct long vowel sound. Then write.

1. p a i l — ay — 2. gr a y
3. pl a y — ai — 4. r a i n
5. t a i l — cr a y on

Listen and choose the correct word.

1. pie / (pay) / pet
2. net / rail / (nail)
3. (tray) / tan / tin
4. say / sand / (sail)

18

Read the name of each picture below. Then write each word in the correct group.

Long ay sound: hay, tray, crayon
Long ai sound: sail, nail, train

train, tray, sail, hay, nail, crayon

Read and circle all the long ay words.

sail plan (pay) mail (tray)
rain (play) ruin (gray) main

Read and circle all the long ai words.

(train) play crayon (tail) clay
(sail) hay May day (rain)

MINI TEST Write the long ay or the long ai word in each blank correctly.

1. He colors a pail gray.
2. My dog has a short tail.
3. We play soccer behind the hay.

word box: play, pail, hay, tail

19

Homework Spot

1. Listen. If the picture is correct, write ◯. But if not, write ✕.
   ◯ ✕ ◯

2. Listen and write the missing letters.
   g r a y   r a i n   p a y
   t r a i n   h a y   t a i l

3. Listen and look at the picture. Then choose Yes or No.
   No Yes Yes No

4. Look and complete the sentences.
   The goat hides behind the hay.
   The rabbit has a small tail.

21

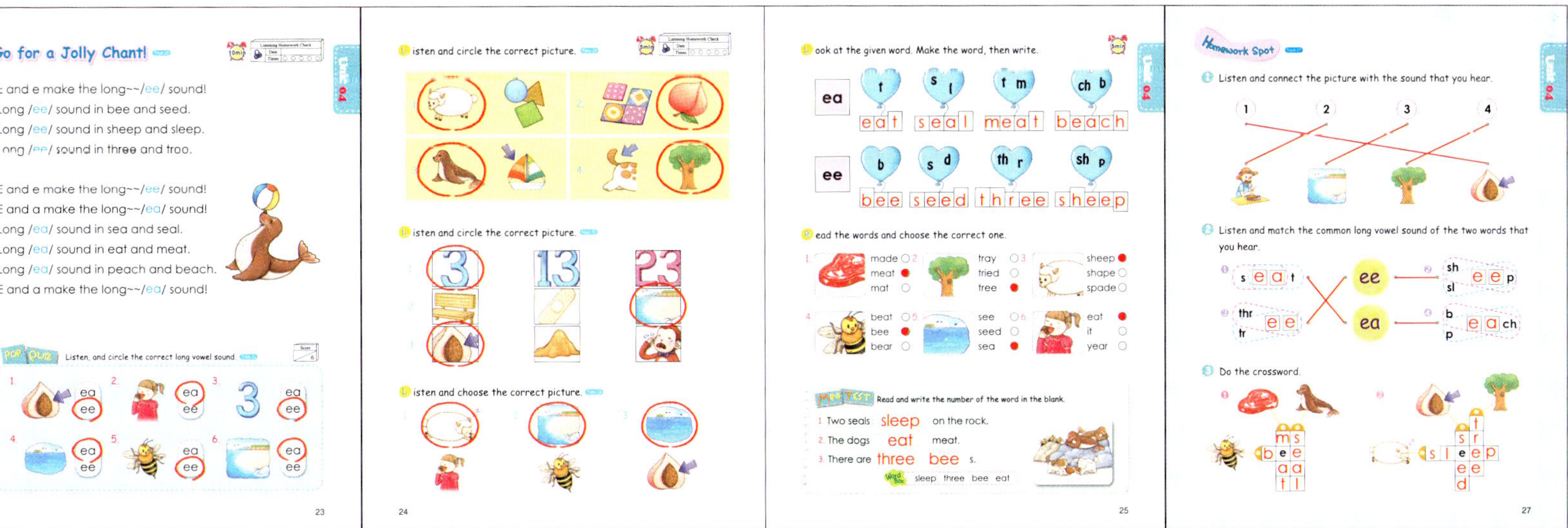

Unit 4

Go for a Jolly Chant!

E and e make the long~~/ee/ sound!
Long /ee/ sound in bee and seed.
Long /ee/ sound in sheep and sleep.
Long /ee/ sound in three and tree.

E and e make the long~~/ee/ sound!
E and a make the long~~/ea/ sound!
Long /ea/ sound in sea and seal.
Long /ea/ sound in eat and meat.
Long /ea/ sound in peach and beach.
E and a make the long~~/ea/ sound!

POP QUIZ Listen, and circle the correct long vowel sound.

1. ea / (ee)   2. (ea) / ee   3. ea / (ee)
4. ea / (ee)   5. (ea) / ee   6. ea / (ee)

23

Listen and circle the correct picture.

Listen and circle the correct picture.

Listen and choose the correct picture.

24

Look at the given word. Make the word, then write.

ea: s t — eat   s l — seal   t m — meat   ch b — beach
ee: b — bee   s d — seed   th r — three   sh p — sheep

Read the words and choose the correct one.

1. made / meat ● / mat
2. tray / tried / tree
3. sheep ● / shape / spade
4. beat / bee ● / bear
5. see / seed / sea ●
6. eat ● / it / year

MINI TEST Read and write the number of the word in the blank.

1. Two seals sleep on the rock.
2. The dogs eat meat.
3. There are three bee s.

word box: sleep, three, bee, eat

25

Homework Spot

1. Listen and connect the picture with the sound that you hear.
   1 2 3 4

2. Listen and match the common long vowel sound of the two words that you hear.
   s e a t — ee — sh / sl — e e p
   thr / tr — e e — ea — b — e a ch — p

3. Do the crossword.
   m s / b e e / a a / t l
   s r / s l e e p / e e / d

27

Unit 5

Unit 6

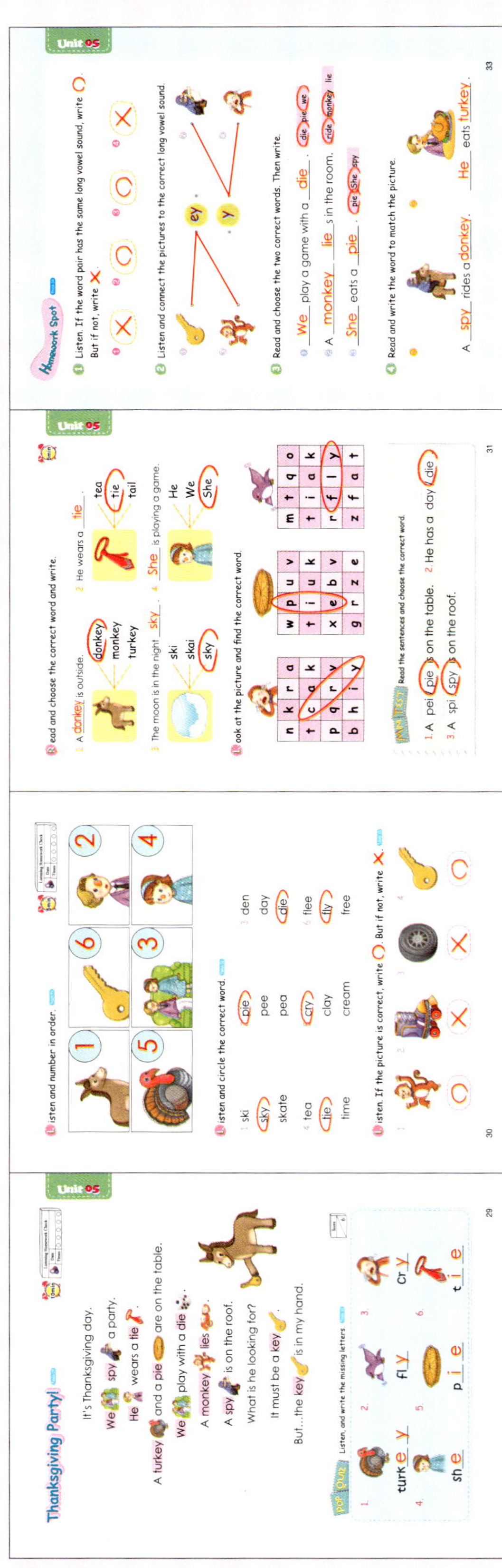

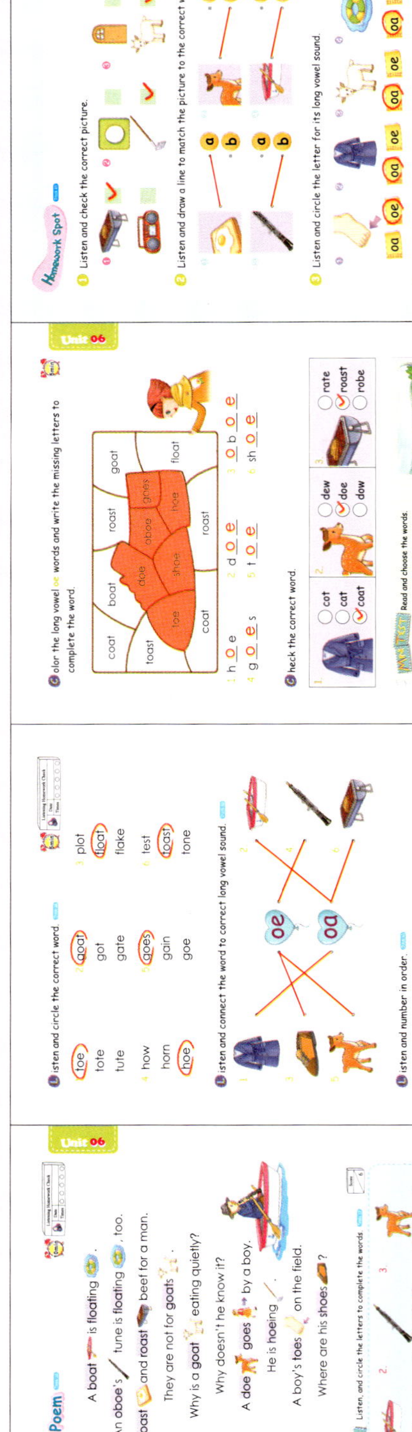

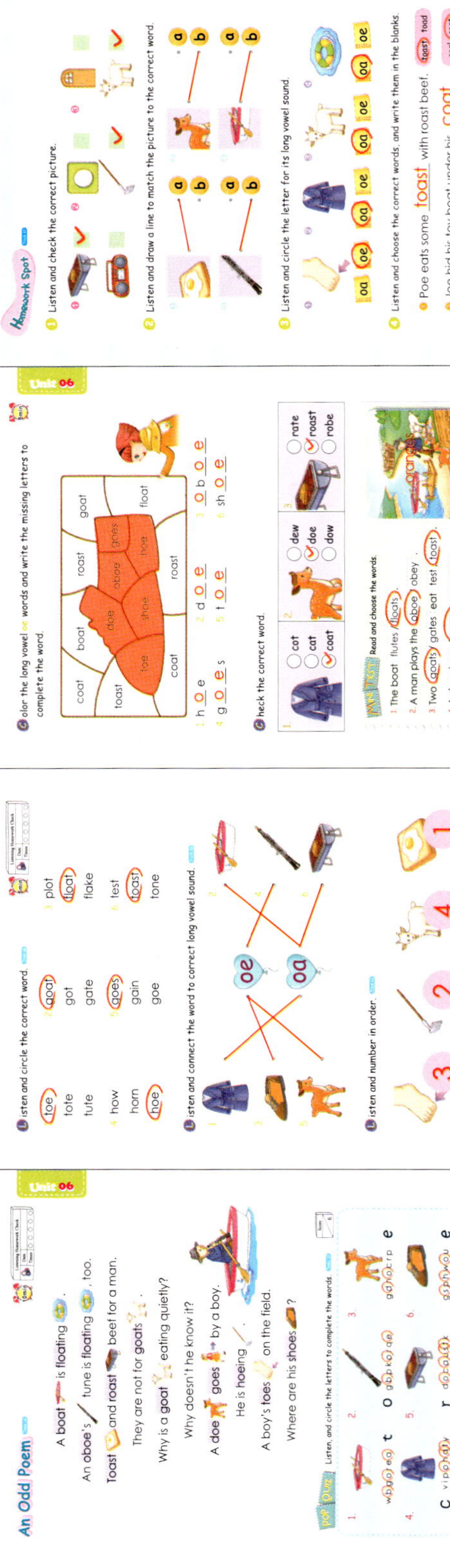

Unit 7

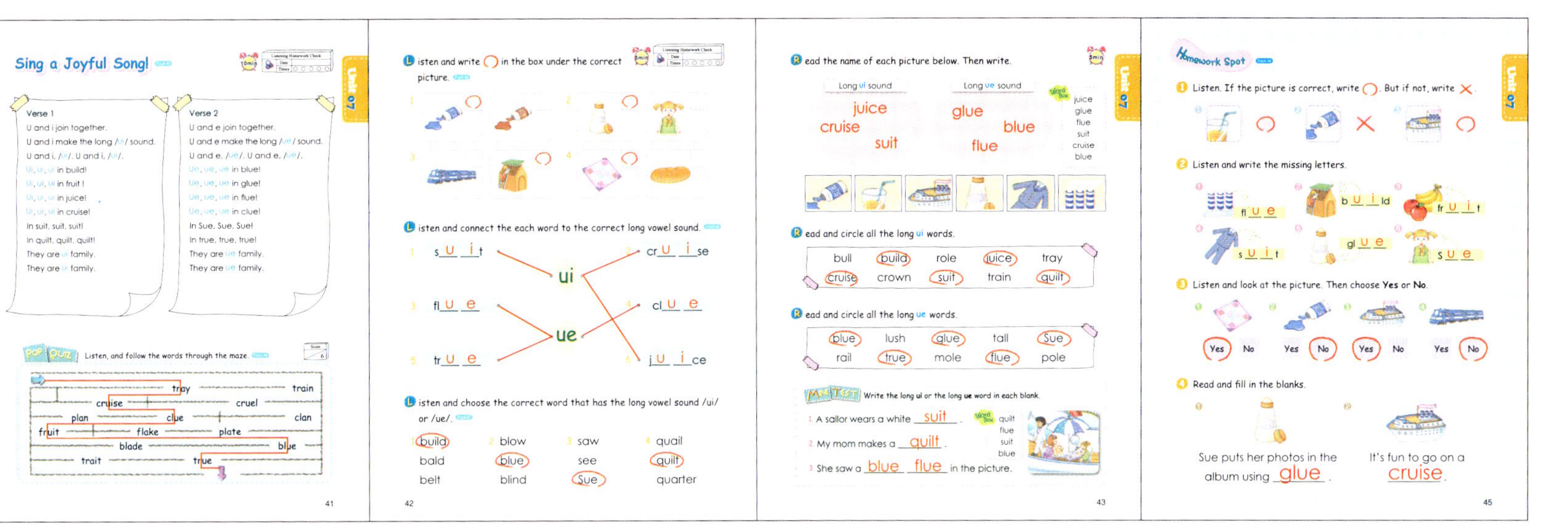

Sing a Joyful Song!
Verse 1
U and i join together.
U and i make the long /ui/ sound.
U and i, /ui/. U and i, /ui/.
Ui, ui, ui in build!
Ui, ui, ui in fruit !
Ui, ui, ui in juice!
Ui, ui, ui in cruise!
In suit, suit, suit!
In quilt, quilt, quilt!
They are ui family.
They are ui family.

Verse 2
U and e join together.
U and e make the long /ue/ sound.
U and e, /ue/. U and e, /ue/.
Ue, ue, ue in blue!
Ue, ue, ue in glue!
Ue, ue, ue in flue!
Ue, ue, ue in clue!
In Sue, Sue, Sue!
In true, true, true!
They are ue family.
They are ue family.

POP QUIZ   Listen, and follow the words through the maze.
tray — train
cruise — cruel
plan — clue — clan
fruit — flake — plate
blade — blue
trait — true
41

Listen and write ◯ in the box under the correct picture.
42

Read the name of each picture below. Then write.
Long ui sound   Long ue sound
juice   glue
cruise   blue
suit   flue
juice / glue / flue / suit / cruise / blue

Read and circle all the long ui words.
bull build role juice tray
cruise crown suit train quilt

Read and circle all the long ue words.
blue lush glue tall Sue
rail true mole flue pole

MINI TEST Write the long ui or the long ue word in each blank.
1. A sailor wears a white suit.
2. My mom makes a quilt.
3. She saw a blue flue in the picture.
43

Listen and connect the each word to the correct long vowel sound.
1 s u i t   cr u i se
   ui
2 fl u e   cl u e
   ue
3 tr u e   j u i ce

Listen and choose the correct word that has the long vowel sound /ui/ or /ue/.
1 build   blow   saw   quail
  bald   blue   see   quilt
  belt   blind Sue   quarter

Homework Spot
1 Listen. If the picture is correct, write ◯. But if not, write ✗.
◯ ◯ ✗ ◯
2 Listen and write the missing letters.
fl u e   b u i ld   fr u i t
s u i t   gl u e   s u e
3 Listen and look at the picture. Then choose Yes or No.
Yes No   Yes No   Yes No   Yes No
4 Read and fill in the blanks.
Sue puts her photos in the album using glue.
It's fun to go on a cruise.
45

Unit 8

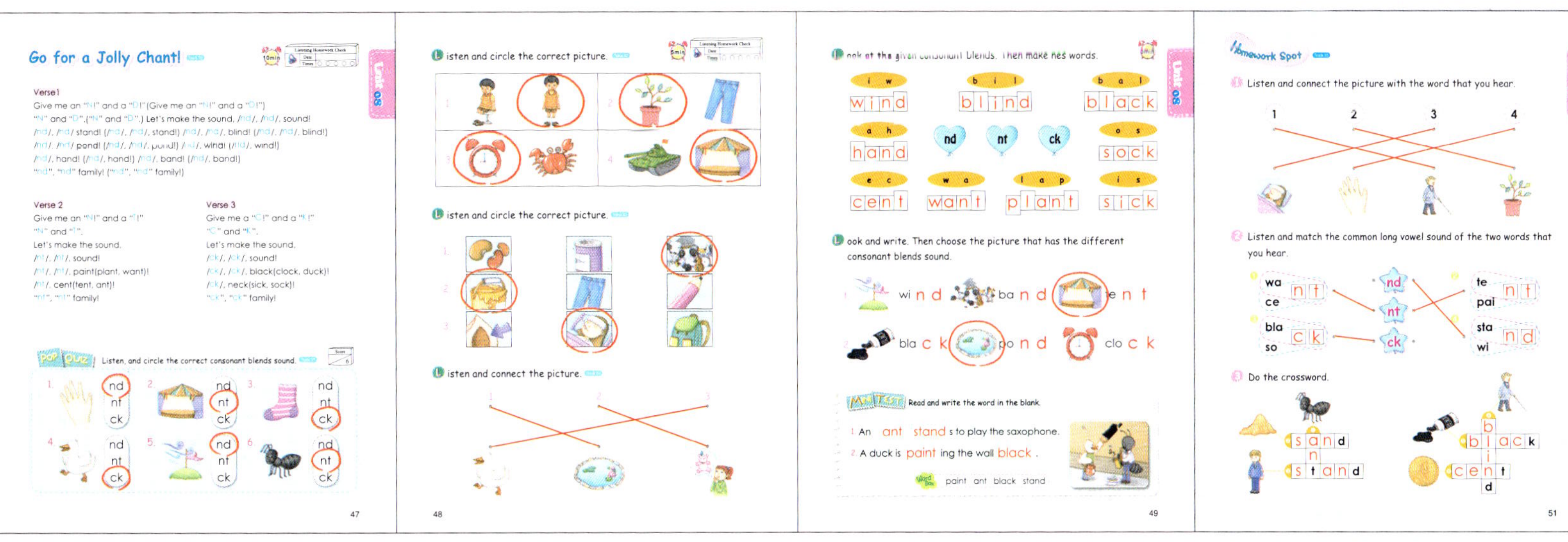

Go for a Jolly Chant!
Verse 1
Give me an "n" and a "d" (Give me an "n" and a "d")
"n" and "d","n" and "d". Let's make the sound, /nd/, /nd/, sound!
/nd/, /nd/ stand! /nd/, /nd/, band! /nd/, /nd/, blind!
/nd/, /nd/ pond! /nd/, /nd/, pond! /nd/, wind! /nd/, wind!
/nd/, /nd/, hand! /nd/, hand! /nd/, band! /nd/, band!
"nd", "nd" family! "nd", "nd" family!

Verse 2
Give me an "n" and a "t"
"n" and "t".
Let's make the sound.
/nt/, /nt/, sound!
/nt/, /nt/, paint(plant, want)!
/nt/, cent(tent, ant)!
"nt", "nt" family!

Verse 3
Give me a "c" and a "k"
"c" and "k".
Let's make the sound,
/ck/, /ck/, sound!
/ck/, /ck/, black(clock, duck)!
/ck/, neck(sick, sock)!
"ck", "ck" family!

POP QUIZ Listen, and circle the correct consonant blends sound.
1 nd nt ck   2 nd nt ck   3 nd nt ck
4 nd nt ck   5 nd nt ck   6 nd nt ck
47

Listen and circle the correct picture.
Listen and circle the correct picture.
Listen and connect the picture.
48

Look at the given consonant blends. Then make nes words.
i w   b i l   b a l
wind   blind   black
a h   nd nt ck   o s
hand   sock
e c   w a   l a p   i s
cent   want   plant   sick

Look and write. Then choose the picture that has the different consonant blends sound.
wi n d ba n d ce n t
bla c k po n d clo c k

MINI TEST Read and write the word in the blank.
1. An ant stands to play the saxophone.
2. A duck is painting the wall black.
paint ant black stand
49

Homework Spot
1 Listen and connect the picture with the word that you hear.
1 2 3 4
2 Listen and match the common long vowel sound of the two words that you hear.
wa nt   te nt
ce   pai
bla ck nd   sta nd
so   nt   wi
3 Do the crossword.
s a n d
s t a n d
b l a c k
c e n t
51

Unit 9

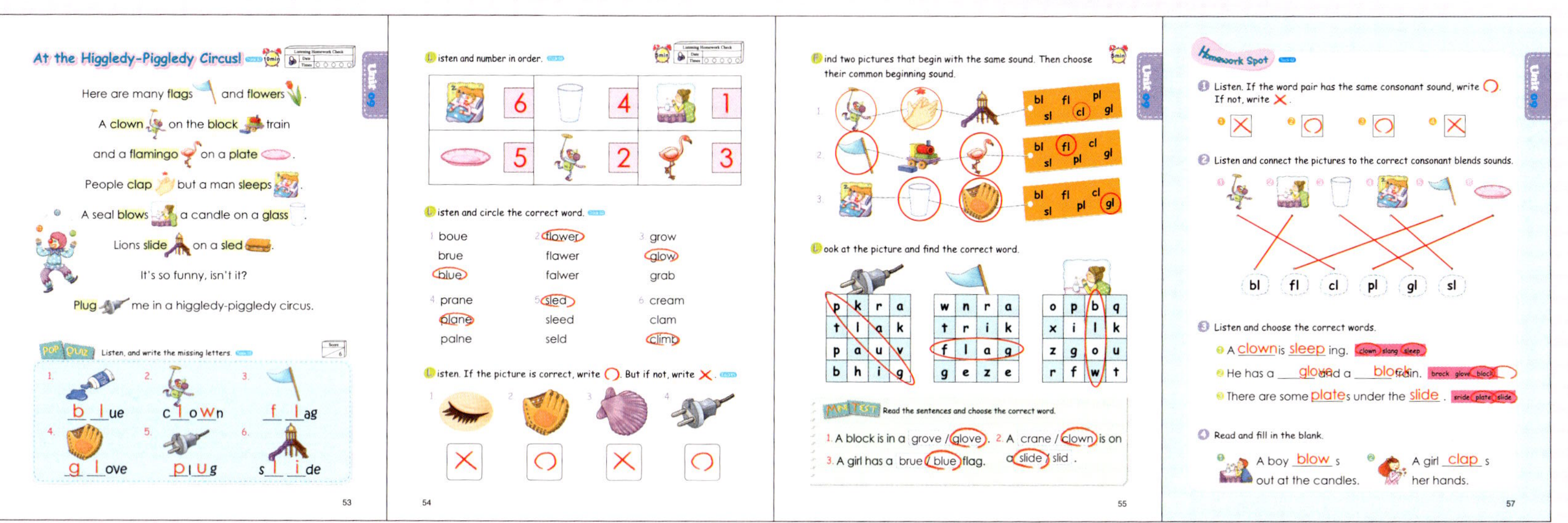

Unit 10

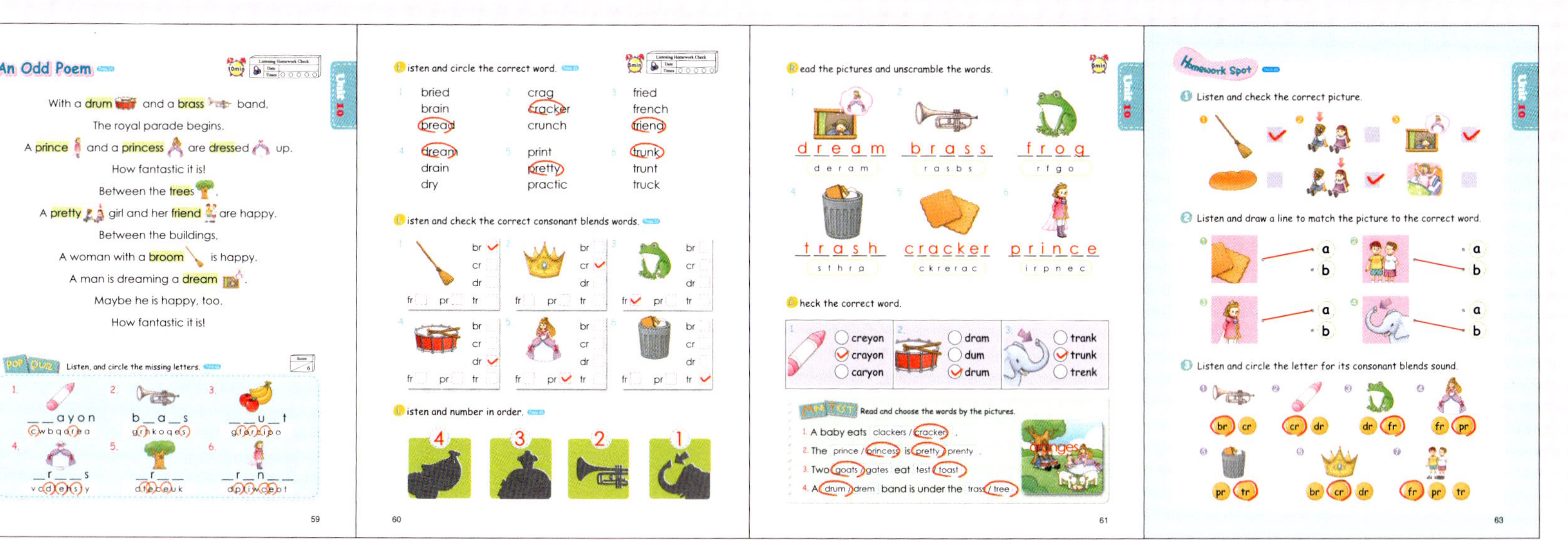

Unit 11

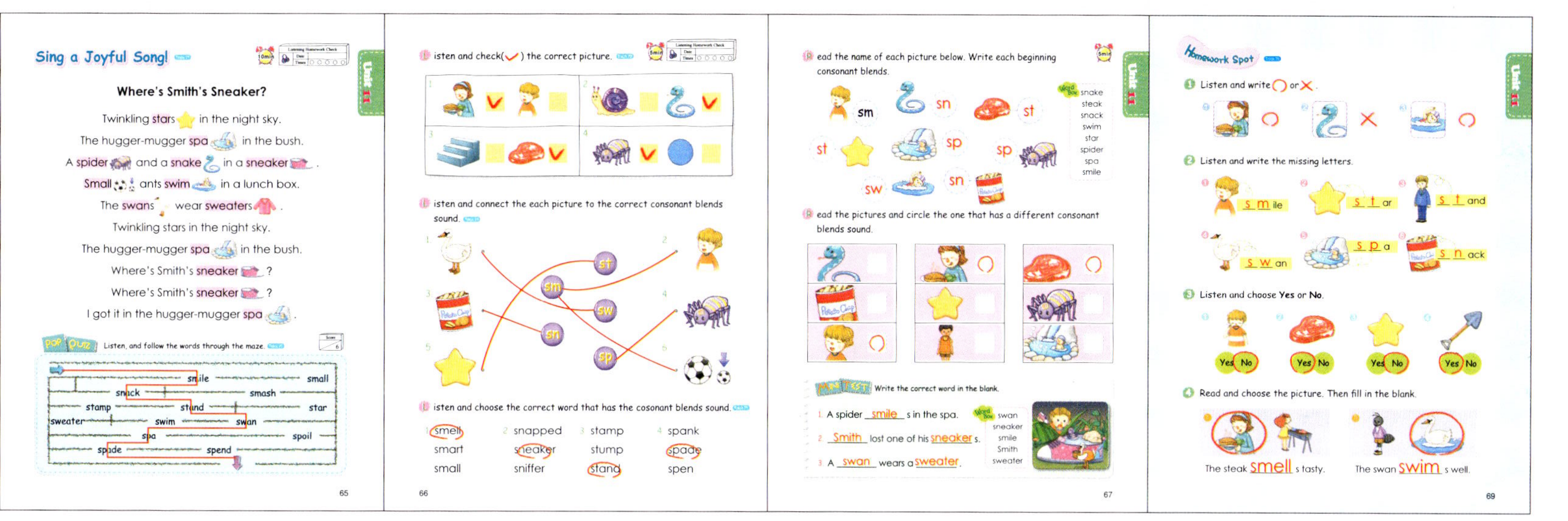

Unit 12

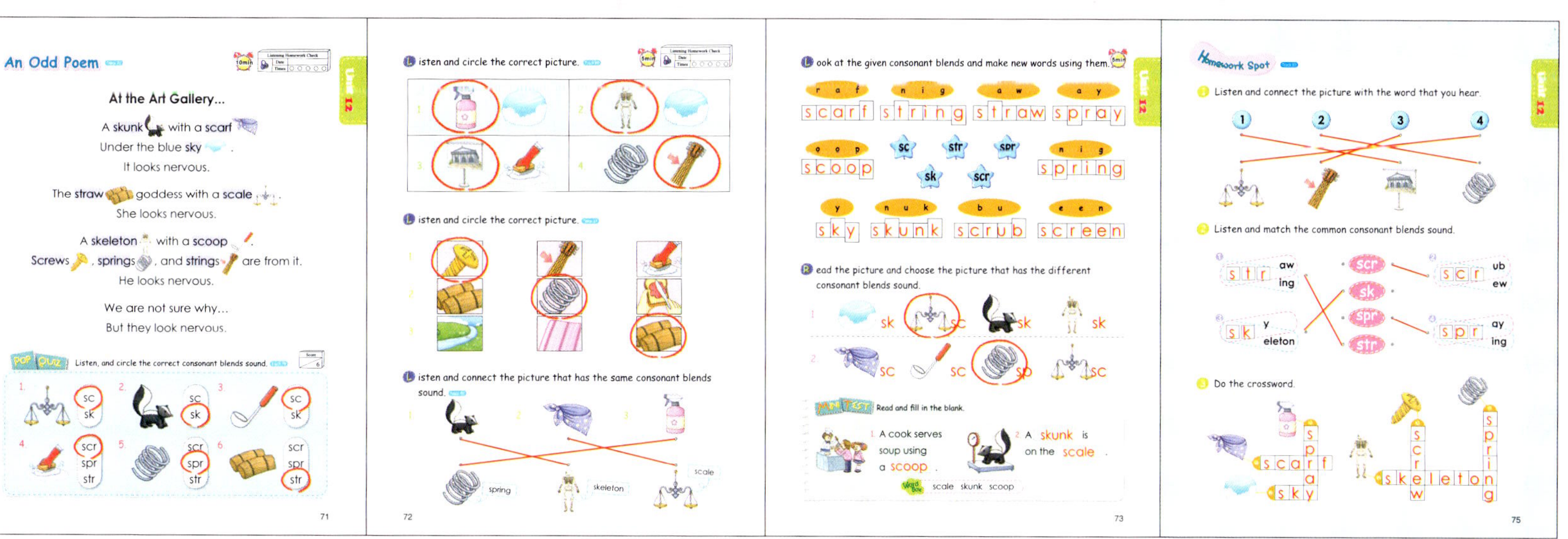

 ant
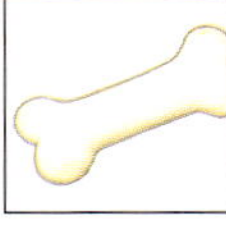 bone
 clown

 band
 brass
 clue

 beach
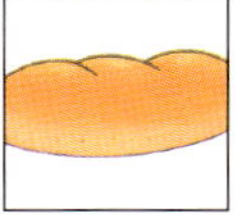 bread
 coat

 bee
 broom
 cone

 bike
 build
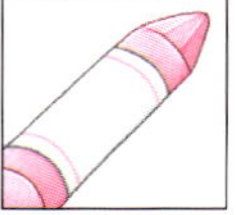 crayon

 blind
 cake
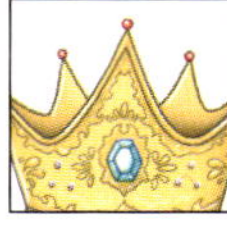 crown

 block
 cave
 cracker

 blow
 cent
 cruise

 blue
 clap
 cry

 black
 climb
 cube

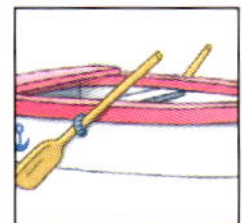 boat
 clock
 cute

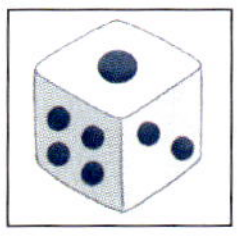

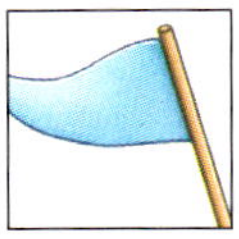

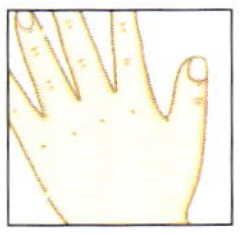

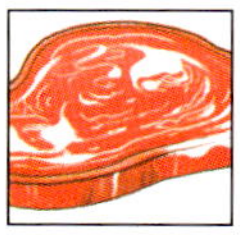

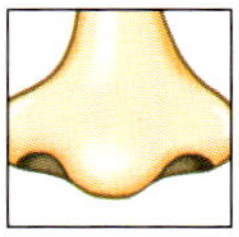

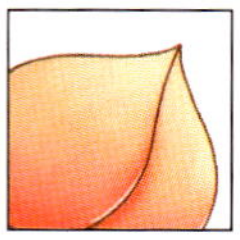

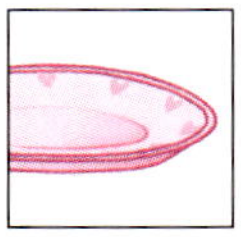

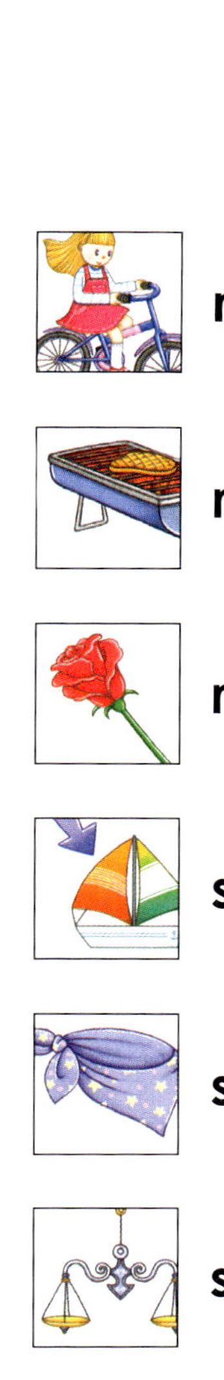

ride	seal	sleep
roast	seed	slide
rose	she	smile
sail	shoe	smell
scarf	sheep	small
scale	sick	snake
scoop	skate	sneaker
scrub	skeleton	snack
screen	skunk	sock
screw	sky	spider
sea	sled	spa

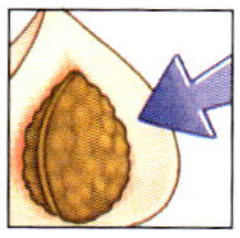

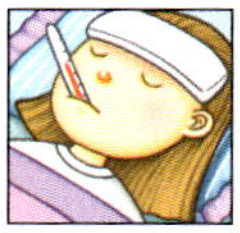

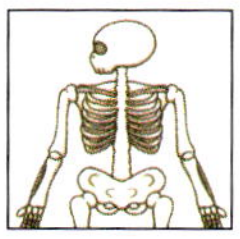

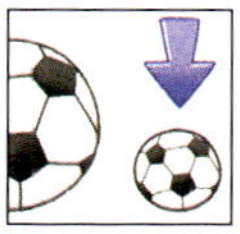

 spade

 swim

 train

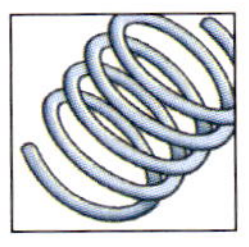 spring

 swan

 tree

 spray

 sweater

 true

 spy

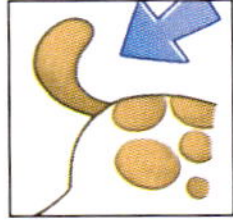 tail

 trunk

 star

 tent

 turkey

 stand

 three

 want

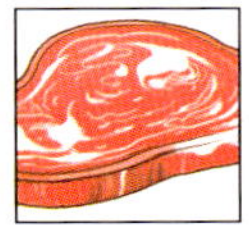 steak

 tie

 wave

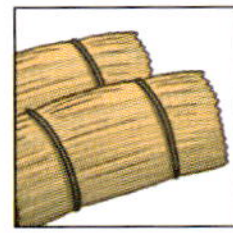 straw

 toast

 we

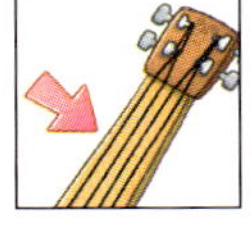 string

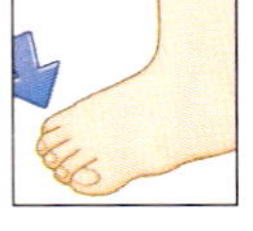 toe

 wind

 suit

 trash

 Sue

 tray

Publication	2011.04.25
Author	Joy Park
Supervisor	LittleLambSchool English Research Institute
Illustration	Joo-Hi Jeong
Publisher	Ki-Seon Lee
Publishing Company	JPlus Publishing Co.
Address	467-30 Mangwon-dong, Mapo-gu, Seoul 121-826, Korea
Telephone	02-332-8320, 02-3142-2520
Fax	02-332-8321
Web site	www.jplus114.com
Registration Number	10-1680
Registration Date	1998. 12. 09
ISBN	978-89-92215-68-8